# The Complete Book of Demonolatry

by S. Connolly

# The Complete Book of Demonolatry

## by S. Connolly

**DB Publishing**
United States of America

DB Publishing is an imprint of Darkerwood Publishing Group, PO Box 2011, Arvada, CO 80001. Contact the publisher for bulk purchases and discounts or contact ofs.admin@gmail.com for online wholesale purchase links.

Parts of this book were first published as:
Modern Demonolatry, Darkerwood Publishing Group 1997
Modern Demonolatry, DB Publishing, 2005
Lessons in Demonolatry, DB Publishing, 2005

Library of Congress-in-Publication Data

Connolly, S., 2006
    The Complete Book of Demonolatry
    I. Occult, II. Demonology, III. Demonolatry
        Bibliography and Indexed
ISBN: 978-0-9669788-6-5

Book Design by DB Publishing, Adrianna.
Cover Art: Steven Lafitte
Foreword by M. Delaney

Printed in the United States of America.

*Warning:* No incenses or oleums contained in this book should be taken internally. DB Publishing and S. Connolly are not responsible for any person using the incenses or oleums improperly in a way that might cause personal injury, illness, or death. Poisonous herbs used in some of the traditional recipes included are clearly marked and should not be taken internally. *DISCLAIMER:* The information in this book is provided for information purposes only. The author and publisher are not responsible for any person who uses the information in this book for illegal activities or if any person is injured or harmed by use of the information contained herein.

# Dedication

This book is dedicated to the family sects for all the information and encouragement they've provided over the years. Especially Mike, who agreed to write the foreword for this book. Likewise, I'd like to thank all the members of OFS who supported and helped with this project – you're all my extended family. And finally I'd like to thank the numerous Demonolators out there, and the many forum members, who tested and tried the lessons in this book and asked the questions that needed to be asked so that the answers could be found. This book is for all of you. May you find wisdom, truth, and always be blessed by the Nine Divinities. Hail Leviathan!

# Contents

# Foreword

When I heard about this book I was excited. Modern Demonolatry was a fine book and Lessons in Demonolatry was nice, too. Putting both of them together with even more information was an excellent idea. I've often used the other two books for training our initiates and I look forward to using this book in the same way.

As a member of one of the "family sects", as we call them, I think it is important to point out that we have been thrilled to find there are others out there like us beyond our own families and groups. We are happy to have offered up some of our information contained within these pages to all of you, but I think it is important to share with all of you why we don't put our family records on display, publish them, or share everything. Most of all, I should share why we are so secretive.

On the first point, you must understand that our family grimoires are also journals and contain some rather personal information about our families. Some of this personal information is personal for a reason. After all, who wants to share with the world that his great-grandmother, for example, practiced perverse blood sex-magic, or that her great-great grandfather had several mistresses? Or, in my case, my great grandmother's shopping lists or recipes for her sister's terrible pecan pie? Yes, that's right. The grimoires are also journals that contain private thoughts and feelings meant only for family and no one else. By publishing these things we would be disrespecting the dead and selling out our own families. Had they intended to share this private information with the world, they likely would have done it themselves, or there would be more than one copy of each journal/grimoire in existence. To add to that, you must also understand that some of the journals, in my case at least, are in German, we think, and other parts are in code. We are still in the process of translating some of it. Some of our journals date back to the 1500's and are currently in the process of being restored. Much of the information about Demonolatry concerning rites, recipes, and Demons, is dispersed throughout and among personal journal entries. Much of what Demonolatry was has been lost due to the lack of a written historical record. Maybe the Demons wanted it that way.

You have to understand that I do not know a life without Demonolatry. Much of what I know doesn't come from grimoires at all. It comes from being raised within the religion and being taught through word-of-mouth from my father who learned from his father and so on. Some of the traditions we practiced on holidays like decorating the house with sigils and putting up special altars for certain Demons during different times of the year are just things my family has always done. It's the way my children have always done things, and hopefully how their children will do things.

On the second matter of privacy, this should be something that we all practice. In the first place there aren't too many of us. My guess is generational Demonolators number under 200 people. That is people who were born and raised in a Demonolatry household. Some people have guessed higher and others lower. The point is we don't know.

Unfortunately Demon Worship has never been a socially acceptable practice in the Christian dominated world we live in. It still isn't. Many of us stand to lose jobs and possibly even our children if we come out with our religious beliefs. Many of us don't participate as much in online Demonolatry communities either because we are busy with our own lives and sects. While that may not seem fair to all of you, I think I speak for all of us who were raised Demonolators when I say the best we can do is offer up what information we can so that you can have some traditional practices to work from. Then you can take your beliefs and raise your children and start your own family groups. Or perhaps you want to keep your Demonolatry practice to yourself, which is okay, too.

It isn't really important that we aren't putting ourselves in the spotlight or that we choose not to share everything from our family grimoires. Some of you may disagree but you may wish to re-evaluate your priorities. What *is* important is the important parts, the basic foundation and some of our traditions *are* being dispersed to all of you through the work of S. Connolly, who has taken a lot of condemnation and criticism for our lack of visibility over the years. She has taken the criticism in stride, and has continued on despite it. I find that admirable.

It is her work and these books that will go down in history's written record as the beginning of Demonolatry even though this book comes five hundred years after the first existing written records we can document. She deserves the credit for bringing Demonolatry from the darkness and into the light so that others may find their way to the wisdom and spirituality of themselves, the Demons, Satan, and a connection to all that is.

If you want definitive proof that Demonolatry is powerful, effective, and can transform your life both spiritually and physically, I dare you to take to heart what this book offers. Those who practice Demonolatry know its power. It's that and that alone that can prove to you that Demonolatry comes from something more ancient and timeless than any five-hundred-year-old grimoire. The Demons existed long before we did. We Demonolators have just perfected the methods in which to commune and work with them peaceably and in friendship to transform ourselves.

In the Light of Lucifer and Baalberith, I remain,

-*M. Delaney*

# About This Book

This book was originally several. The first was Modern Demonolatry, which I never felt was complete. I had considered revising it for some time, but then realized I had so much to add that I should write a book that included all the new material I had written plus all the information in Lessons in Demonolatry. Initially, DB Publishing wanted to do a training series of books that would help Demonolators from Pre-Initiate, to Initiate, to Adept, but it seemed silly, and a waste of time to repeat the same information over and over again. Not to mention it seemed impractical to keep writing separate books for each topic, especially for the Demonolator or Theistic Satanist who just wanted one book that covered all the basics through adepthood. Instead, we decided it would be best to write a single book that included all of this information.

This book focuses on the foundation and spiritual side of Demonolatry, and will introduce you to Demonolatry Magick. If you are interested in more information about Demonolatry Magick, you should check out *The Art of Creative Magic or Goetic Demonolatry* by my good friend, Ellen Purswell. That said, I'd also like to take this time to point out that since Modern Demonolatry's initial release in 1999, a good number of Theistic Satanists, Satanic groups, and some Gnostic Luciferians have started working with Demons in a more respectful manner using Demonolatry exclusive Enns, sigils, and practices like dedication rituals. These things were unheard of prior to Demonolatry.com, Tezrian's Vault, and the initial release of Modern Demonolatry in 1999. The consensus, from those who have used these particular Demonolatry methods, is that they are extremely effective.

This book can be used as a general reference as well as a study guide and workbook for the pre-initiate and initiate. For the adept, this book will give some insight into personal path working, which is the logical next step in your own personal spiritual evolution.

One thing this book does include, that is of extreme significance, is all the sigils for the Dukante hierarchy. We've never put them all out like this before. I have also included all the Goetic hierarchy sigils. While numerous books do include the Goetic hierarchy and the sigils, having one book in front of you can be so much easier than having two or three when you're studying.

While I am calling this book *The Complete Book of Demonolatry*, I'm sure there may be things I've missed. Not many authors would admit that. Truthfully, it would be ludicrous for me to claim that one book could contain every piece of information about a single topic. Firstly, much of Demonolatry has been lost over the years and secondly, there is still a lot buried in private family journals;

information that will likely never see the light of day. That's just how things go.

In lieu of this, you'll find a lot of modern things alongside the older rites in this book. I will let you know what I've written or modified for use here (as opposed to what comes from family grimoires) in the appropriate section. Much of the newer inclusions are my rites and augmentations of certain things from other paths and traditions for use in Demonolatry. I've found that modification is perfectly acceptable and is just as effective because the alleged originals all spring from the same, older source. For those of you who disagree with augmentation to that which already exists, or see it as a perversion of another tradition, this book may not be for you.

I am *not* of the belief that older is better or the *only* valid way. I also don't believe we should only trust things over one hundred years old, or only things that are written down in books. Not even this one. After all, personal experiences and feelings take precedence over the written word when it comes to spirituality. Plus, religion does not exist in a vacuum and must grow and change with the times to reflect new ideas and information. All religions have built upon things of the past, which you'll read about in the history section of this book. So while history is important and the older rites are valid and effective, I think you'll find the newer rites are very powerful and continue to add to our history. Feel free to write your own rites, too.

Now I'd like to directly address the Demonolatry students reading this book. The most important thing you can do during your study and practice of Demonolatry is keep journals. By going back over them a year from now or twenty years from now, you'll be able to see how far you've come. Your journals should contain your thoughts, feelings, experiments, rituals, and experiences with the Demons. You should also record your spiritual revelations and observations.

Demonolatry, first and foremost, is all about *your* personal relationship with the Demons and your personal spiritual growth and connection to all that is. *It's not about Demonic magick*, even though magick can certainly take a large role in self-discovery and positive life change. What I am saying is magick doesn't *have to be* a part of Demonolatry, but it often is.

So now I give you *The Complete Book of Demonolatry*. In Light, Peace, and in honor of the Self and the Demons,

– S. Connolly

# Introduction to Demonolatry

Within the following pages you will find rites of Demonolatry long held clandestine in Satanism's misunderstood history. This is not a book for the light-hearted. Nor is it a book for the casual dabbler. It is meant for use as a Demonology reference, and a practical grimoire for the modern day practitioner of Demonolatry.

First off, I think it is important that the student should know the correct terminology to begin learning about Demonolatry. All too often I hear people referring to Demonolatry as Demonology. Even seasoned occult scholars make this mistake. While both schools focus on the Demon entity, one is the study whilst the other remains the worship and practice. These are two very different schools of thought, indeed.

**Demon/Daemon/Daimon**: Lesser spirit or god. A devil in Christian mythology. Literal meaning for Demon - "Replete with wisdom." Derived from the Greek "daimon" meaning divine power.

**Demonic**: Being as or resembling a Demon.

**Demoniac**: A person possessed by Demons.

**Demonocracy**: The Demonic hierarchies and/or governments.

**Demonographer**: One who studies and records the history and description of Demons.

**Demonography**: The history and description of Demons.

**Demonolator(er)/Demonolatress**: One who practices Demonolatry.

**Demonolatry**: The worship of Demons and/or practicing ritual magick with the aid of entities known as Demons.

**Demonologist**: One who studies and catalogues Demons. Also known as a Demonographer.

**Demonology**: The study and cataloguing of Demons.

**Demonomancy**: Divination by means of Demons according to some texts. Literally "to raise Demons."

**Daemon, Demon, Daemonolatrie, Daemonolatry, Demonolatry, Demonolatrie, Daemonolator, Demonolator, Demonolater:** All of these are just a variety of spellings for the same words. Some people use Daemon, Daemonolator, and Daemonolatry out of respect. Others use all spellings of the term depending on whim. None of them are *wrong*. None of these terms belong to any individual or group. They are simply different incarnations of the same words. Use whichever spelling you wish to use.

**What is Demonolatry?**

It is quite literally - "the worship of Demons." It is, to the modern Demonolator, the practice of calling on elemental or pure energy forces known as Demons to aid in self-knowledge, spiritual growth, and projecting one's will onto an object or person through use of ritual magick. For the theistic Demonolator, Demons are very real entities. Let's look at several definitions of Demonolatry:

This first one is from Grandma Gynna's "What is Demonolatry" originally printed on Demonolatry.com, and ofs-Demonolatry.org and used here, modified by me for further clarification, with permission.

Demonolatry is a religion of the Self. [*Meaning we do Self work to better ourselves.*] It is about discovering the personal divine power within each of us and living within the natural balance of the energies surrounding us [*the Universe*]. It is also about Self-Responsibility and inner peace. Demons, to some, are simply focal points of single pure energies. To others they are real entities with personalities and individual consciousness.

Each of the Demons is the embodiment of an emotion, an element, or an idea. Some people believe these energies are sentient [*real deities*], while others believe they are simply natural forces without consciousness. I know this certainly sounds as Wiccan as it gets, but it really isn't. There are many differences including the base Hermetic foundation of our religion, and we have different Pantheons/Gods. Our Gods are Demons [*Divine Intelligences Replete with Wisdom*] because they represent misunderstood or clandestine parts of the world around us.

Many Demons were merely Gods of pre-Christian pagan religions. There are Demons for love and healing just as sure as there are Demons for anger and destruction. There is a natural balance to our religion [*Hermetic*]. For every Demon, there is an equal and opposite Demon. There are also those Demons on the subtle in-between of the two. In our religious philosophy, everything, every situation, and everyone has this balance. Therefore, we see the world in many subtle shades of gray and consider ourselves the physical manifestations of the divine. Demonolatry does include Self-Worship.

In our religion there is no heaven or hell. Many of us believe in reincarnation of our own personal energies. We also tend to take science into account when it comes to questions like "Where did we come from?" and "Are there other planets like ours in the universe?" and so on. Our religion doesn't conflict with scientific theories about creation, our universe, and evolution.

Within the practice of Demonolatry there are many rites. Most of them are meditative [*and include prayer and mental exercises*], while others incorporate magick in which requests are burnt, incenses and candles are lit representing certain aspects of the ritual's design. Many different forms of magick are used in conjunction with our religion. This depends on the individual's preference. We encourage a personal belief system that fulfills the needs of the practitioner.

A lot of people misconstrue our magickal practices as our religion. Magick is generally what people see on the forefront. What we gain from that practice is inner peace, positive self-image, strength and courage, and a deep-seated knowledge of ourselves, and humanity. Instead of attempting to stare into the eyes of our Gods, we form a personal relationship with them and work with them as our wise teachers and eternal friends. What we hope to achieve is to be able to look *through* the eyes of our Gods. Each and every Demon is a part of us as we are a part of them.

Now we'll take a look at an encyclopedic entry I helped write that describes Demonolatry. Please note that I have modified it in the context of this book for further clarification.

Demonolatry--not to be confused with Demonology (the study of Demons)--means, literally, the worship of Demons. Although the word is old, it was originally used (like the label Satanism) as a term of derision to refer to a variety of different religions that the early Church persecuted. It was not adopted as a term of self-reference until relatively recently (late 1950's/early 1960's). Even then, Demonolatry was clandestine. It was not until 1998 when the Guild of Demonolatry (now defunct) finally funded a website--Tezrian's Vault--devoted to the religion that Demonolatry came out-of-the-closet. That site closed in 2001. Previously, many sects simply referred to themselves as followers of [*insert name of Demon here*].

Modern Demonolatry is a polytheistic or pantheistic religion (depending if you see some Demons above others or all of them equal) in which Demonic entities are worshiped and worked with as wise divinities. Each Demon is the wellspring of a single energy source. These energies can be defined as universal elements, emotions, or ideas. The most common pantheon of Gods used are Demonic-- from Christian mythologies about diabolical beings, which were formerly the Gods of pre-Christian pagan religions. However, Roman, Greek, Egyptian, and other pantheons have been used.

Perhaps the most popular of the pantheons is the Richard Dukante Hierarchy, which was developed in the early 1960's. It became the basis for many modern Demonolatry sects. We're told Dukante created his hierarchy by pulling the names of Demons that appeared across several different family grimoires. For example, since Lucifer was mentioned in all of the grimoires Dukante looked at, he put that Demon on the list. Then he categorized them into families.

Each practitioner of Demonolatry chooses what is known as a "counterpart" Demon, or a Demon that defines or identifies with the attributes of the practitioner. This becomes the individual's matron or patron deity (depending on gender association). All Demons become secondary to this particular Demon. For those practitioners who border on what might be called theistic Satanism, this Demon may or may not be Satan. In Demonolatry, Satan is the "fifth element," or the source of all other energies. In other words, Satan is the Whole and every other Demon is simply a part of the whole. Each person, animal, plant, and thing that exists in nature is a part of the whole [the divine] as well. Because of this, there are no Demons more "powerful" than others.

In worshiping Demons, Demonolaters mean that they respect them and hold them in high regard as teachers and friends. They are not evil, but, rather, are benign. Some Demonolators believe that Demons are simply energy sources, while others believe they are actual entities. This varies from practitioner to practitioner. Regardless of their perspective, Traditional Demonolaters reject Christian mythology about Satan, Demons, heaven or hell, and do not believe in the Christian God.

Most Demonolaters accept that:

1. **Everything in the universe is interconnected.**

2. **There are no such things as absolute good and evil.** Rather, there are many subtle shades of gray.

3. **Demonic entities are teachers/guides and deserve respect.**

4. **Demonolaters do not, therefore, conjure/evoke Demons against the Demon's will.**

5. Satan is the whole, the Demons and ourselves are parts of the whole and therefore also divine.

6. **We are responsible for our every action**, and every action has an equal and opposite reaction.

7. **We create our own reality** (with the aid of the Demons or without it).

8.  **Spiritual growth and self-discovery take place so long as one maintains a personal relationship with one's patron/matron and the whole.** i.e. The Demon is the guide that leads man to his Divine nature.

9.  **Belief, religion, and opinion are unique to each individual and based on individual experiences and ideas.** One does not have to agree with everyone, but rather one should respect others' rights to have their own beliefs, religion, and opinion without judging or condemning them.

Demonolaters do not regard themselves as being in the tradition of Anton LaVey's Satanism, although individual Demonolators may personally believe in some aspect of his philosophy, particularly in the Self Worship aspects. However, LaVey's philosophy is not a driving force behind Demonolatry as a religion. **Demonolatry advocates self-empowerment and spiritual growth through developing a relationship with one's "creator" or the whole, and by discovering one's own purpose, divine nature and power within the scheme of things (or as part of the whole).**

There are two types of Demonolators with regards to practice: those whose approach is primarily religious and those who practice Demonic Magick. Much of modern Demonolatry is steeped in elemental magick. The major religious rites are as follows (the specific dates may vary, but these are the days these holidays generally fall on):

**March 21 - Rite to Lucifer** in celebration of enlightenment and the air that sustains life on this planet. It is also a celebration of knowledge, education, and ideas. It is also a celebration of spring and new beginnings. Marriages are sometimes performed on or around the Rite to Lucifer.

**May 2 - First Rite to Leviathan.** This is typically an initiation ceremony. Leviathan symbolizes the seed cycle and emotional bonds. Many sects choose to initiate their new arrivals during this rite. However, it is also the Rite wherein some people may choose to get married or to conceive children as it symbolizes fertility and bonding.

**June 21 - Rite to Flereous.** Flereous is the Phoenix that rises from the ashes. This rite celebrates the warmth of the sun and summer. This is the Rite at which Baphometic Fire Baptisms are performed. Baptisms are rarely performed on children. However, adults may choose to have their matron or patron deity's sigil either branded, tattooed, or cut somewhere into their body. While some cultures may regard this as self-mutilation, a Demonolator finds honor in this ritual and bears the "scar" proudly. Nowadays, tattoos are very popular because sigils can be encompassed in a picture.

**September 21 - Second Rite to Leviathan**. This is the Rite that celebrates autumn and harvest. It celebrates the element water. It also celebrates emotional ties (married couples sometimes choose this Rite to reaffirm wedding vows). Scrying, tarot readings, and other forms of divination are practiced during this time as it is believed that the connection between the many parts of the whole are stronger now.

**October 31 - Rite to Eurynomous**. Also honored are Baalberith and Babael. This rite, as in many other traditions, is a celebration of death, dying, and the dead.

Many people choose this rite to "destroy" bad feelings by requesting curses on those who have wronged them. Cursing rites are a condoned and encouraged practice in Demonolatry. This is a time of emotional cleansing and self-renewal.

**December 21 - Rite to Belial**. This is sometimes called the second initiation rite because Belial also represents new beginnings. Belial represents material things, financial matters, and business endeavors. It is the celebration of winter, family and friends, and the birth of the sun (as it is the shortest day of the year).

These are the principal rites practiced by religious Demonolators in addition to the holiday of their Patron/Matron deity. They are too numerous to list. [*Added*] However, many people have asked about the Rites of Belphegore and the Second Rite to Lucifer. The **second Rite to Lucifer** falls on November 13th. The **Rites to Belphegore** fall on March 31st, April 9th, and May 13th. We also found **Lucifuge Rofocal's holy day** was of interest to people. That date is September 14th.

Demonolators who practice Demonic magick also participate in the above holidays, but they will formulate rites in which to work magick whenever the need suits them. Unlike witchcraft of other forms of folk magick, Demonic magick generally only happens within the confines of a structured ritual or rite. Circles are constructed for containing and balancing the "energy" rather than protection. Incenses, herbal mixtures, and focusing materials are often used. Ritual oils for anointing candles and people are also common. Blood Rites, in which the practitioner cuts herself and uses her own blood during ritual, is a regular part of many older rituals. It should be noted that for blood rites practitioners are taught to take blood in the least destructive way possible (e.g., pricking a finger, menstrual blood for women, and so on). Self-mutilation in not a part of Demonolatry.

Demonolatry has formal marriage rites (conducted in the name of Rosier and the patron/matron), formal funeral services (conducted in the name of the matron or patron, Eurynomous, Baalberith, and Babael), and formal divorces (in the name of the matron/patron and Rosier or Satan).

Religious Demonolators use prayer for self-empowerment while those who practice Demonic magick use both prayer and magick for self- empowerment. To those who use Demonic magick, the magick itself is symbolic and helps to focus personal energy to create a change in one's life. Many Demonolators believe that magick has a scientific explanation that we have yet to uncover.

Hopefully these more in-depth explanations of Demonolatry have helped you to understand the nature and scope of Demonolatry as a religion.

### Isn't Satan just a part of Christian Mythology?

Well, yes and no. The name - Satan - means adversary. This is something akin to Lucifer, who - prior to Christian perversion - was a god whose name meant The Light Bringer. He was a pre-Christian pagan sun god. Most of Christianity's Demons are dark (and sometimes not so dark) gods of pre-Christian religions. Demonolators worship these gods because they embody the darker side of nature, which we sometimes do not understand. They are the elements by which we were created. We worship them as our creators. The gods of the past are indicative of what humanity will become. (That is, enlightened. We hope.)

**Do Demonolators See and Speak With Demons?**

Some say yes and others say no. This depends on who you're talking to and what they believe. I, personally, do believe that Demons sometimes physically manifest. I also believe they communicate with us. Sometimes that communication is subtle, and other times it's outright. Mind you I am not talking about hearing voices, but rather having a sudden thought that comes from nowhere, but that contains sound advice. Note that Demons are different than devils. Devils signify malevolence. Demons are neither evil nor good, as Christian Mythology will have us believe. They are shades of gray. Everything good can cause something negative and vice versa.

**Why are Demonolators not Satanists?**

Well, they are and can be by definition. However, some Satanists refuse to acknowledge them as such. In recent years, however, many theistic Satanists have embraced the Demonolatry subculture. Modern Satanists do not believe in the Demon entity - even in the form of an energy with physical properties. Some Luciferians will tell you that they are modern Demonolators by definition. Others will claim no such attachment. Demonolators are, essentially, theistic Satanists to some degree. The difference is that Satan is not necessarily the patron/primary deity. Most Demonolators end up worshipping their elemental Demon.

**How Come Satan isn't the Patron deity?**

Demonolatry requires that each practitioner select a counterpart Demon. This counterpart becomes the patron or matron deity. There are two ways to define a Demon. A Demon is an entity with its own mind and agenda. A Demon is literally - a focus point of a single pure energy. People give them names and attributes so that we can identify with them, visualize them, and work with them. Demons are not worshipped by most *modern* Demonolators (those who see Demons as energies instead of beings) they are "worked with." The reason for this is because Demons are seen as energies by these people, and one cannot worship an energy. So when a modern Demonolator says to you: " I've never worshipped my electrical box..." you'll understand why.

On the other hand, traditional or theistic Demonolators do worship the Demons (actual entities) that embody attributes of the practitioner. This is not limited to Satan.

### Is Demonolatry a form of Magick, a Religion, or a Philosophy?

Unlike modern LaVeyan Satanism, which is merely a philosophy with added ritual magick, Demonolatry is primarily a religion, but can encompass magickal practice. There is a lot of room for expanding and personalizing Demonolatry to the practitioner's lifestyle. As magick and religion are independent of one another, magick can be added to the practice Demonolatry (as has been done throughout the ages). But the practice of magick is not required.

### Do Demonolators Do Ritual Sacrifices?

No. Most Demonolators do not condone physical sacrifice (as in killing), ritual or other, of any animal or person. Of course emotional and indirect sacrifice of adult people is fully supported with just cause. Usually a working of magick where the end goal is death will suffice. And, as always, there really has to be a good reason for wanting to curse, let alone kill, someone in the first place. Some sects might practice chicken sacrifice. Once they sacrifice the bird, they will cook and eat it at a feast following the rite.

Let me point out here that the word "sacrifice" means, "to make sacred".

I would like to share my thoughts on this subject. **The following is the author's opinion**: Some people feel sacrifice is a powerful thing, appreciated by the Demons. I think an entity respects the practitioner who is willing to sacrifice his own blood before that of another creature. I don't mean committing suicide. I simply mean that a few drops of one's own blood is more potent than killing an innocent creature because it comes from *you*. I respect others beliefs though, and do believe that if the creature is to be consumed at a feast following the rite, then at least it's a respectful sacrifice. I am of the opinion that killing just for the blood is pointless if you have no intention of consuming the flesh of the sacrifice. Sacrifice means to "make sacred". And that means, in my humble opinion, that no creature should suffer in the act of making it's death sacred. In which case the creature being sacrificed should be killed as quickly and painlessly as possible. After all, if I was part of the food chain and I were to be sacrificed, I'd want to be respected enough to be killed quickly, and honored for giving up my life. In the very least my body could be used to nourish those who sacrificed me, after my demise.

Still, I personally could not stomach killing a chicken, let alone any other living thing. It's just not for me. I'd much rather use my own blood.

**So what is it the Demon gets from the practitioner?**
When you worship, respect, or hold anyone or thing in high regard, there is a transference of healthy, positive energy. This is what the Demon gets from the practitioner. Relax - there's no selling your soul, or fire and brimstone for eternity. These things are merely perpetuated myths

handed down from a religion long past its prime. Commonly, popular literature like Marlowe's Dr. Faustus and Dante's renowned Divine Comedy - Inferno are what people envision when they think of Demon worship.

### Getting Rid of a Christian Viewpoint of the Demonic.

Usually, losing the Christian viewpoint of Demons comes naturally for those who practice Demonolatry. Just remember that Demons are not the ugly little red beasties with horns, tails, and pitchforks of Christian Mythology. They appear as the practitioner wishes them to appear. Some say that if you saw a Demon in its natural form, it looks no different than a brilliant colored light. The philosopher Goethe said the Daimonic was nature. Many Greek philosophers said they had personal Daimon and referred to the nature of Daimon. (Divine Intelligence) So if you always remember that there is history before Christianity, and that Demons were around long before Christianity became an established religion, then you will eventually drop the Christian viewpoint of Demons. Some people have written themselves rituals that they use to get rid of the dogma engrained in them from their Christian upbringings. You can find such a ritual, created by J. Caven, in the book *Demonolatry Rites*.

Along with this loss of Christian viewpoint will come a different viewpoint of the world in general. Things are no longer black and white, but rather shades of gray. This is because after practicing Demonolatry, learning from Demons, and spiritual growth, we begin to see that even the positive has a negative side and vice versa.

### Is Demonolatry Right Hand Path or Left Hand Path?

(This question was taken from the FAQ on our website when the question kept coming up and people just weren't getting it.)

Ah, the long debated question as to whether or not a person can be theistic and still take responsibility for him/herself. We have recently decided the RHP and LHP definitions are so screwy that trying to define ourselves as LHP or RHP is moot. We are of the Demonolatry Path. Maybe it meets somewhere in the middle, I don't know, nor do I think I care now that a friend has enlightened me.

However, many consider us LHP because Traditional Demonolators believe we are all parts of the whole and thus no less than Gods ourselves (even though imperfect by our very nature). We're simply bound by the physical body.

Self-knowledge, Self-responsibility, and Self-Worship are all parts of Demonolatry as is the quest for knowledge and the practice of Demon worship. We do not grovel before the Demons as unworthy beings that depend on their aide to do anything. They do not control us. We control ourselves. We work with the Demons and honor them to discover our true potential as imperfect yet divine beings bound by a physical plane of existence. By honoring and worshiping them we are honoring and worshiping ourselves because they are a part of us as we are a part of them. All things are divine. We don't spend our time trying to look into the eyes of our gods. Instead, we work toward looking through the eyes of our Gods. Basically, we are all the physical manifestation of the divine.

We define worship as reverence and respect and to *hold in high regard.*

## The Demonic Entity & the Concept of Deity

The three most common ways in which the Demon is seen

- 1. As in Christian mythology. Tempters who lead men against God in sin.
- 2. As a single, pure energy source anthropomorphized by names and attributes.
- 3. As gods in their own right as Demon means divine power or a being replete with wisdom.

Of course many personal views reflect that a Demon is some aspect of what we know as (or to be) deity. Most people believe a deity is merely who or what we worship. There are also several concepts of deity.

- 1. The divine force we worship as we are at its mercy.
- 2. The divine force whose wisdom we trust in.
- 3. As a divine force we respect and choose to work with harmoniously. Which means we respect the deity by paying homage to it (worship).

Demonolatry is "Demon Worship" with numbers 2 & 3 as definitions of the Entity and the Deity. This comprises the basic concept of Demonolatry.

By now you must have a good idea of what you're in for. So let's move on and delve further into Demons.

# All About Demons

In this section you will learn about Demonic Hierarchies, creating personal pantheons, the purposes of Demons, the Dukante hierarchy, the Enns, and the sigils.

Please be aware that the various hierarchies are included, compiled from sources listed in the back of the book, to show you how people have catalogued Demons over the past 500-1000 years. I make no claims to accuracy regarding these hierarchies nor their authors. I am simply repeating lists as they've appeared in numerous books. I have made notes where certain lists are concerned regarding any new information I've come across regarding origin. For this I thank the numerous occult scholars who have corrected me. In some cases I have relied on their word. If you are interested in a particular Demon or hierarchy, I highly advise you research it yourself for historical accuracy. Unfortunately I do not have the means or skills to go visit the libraries housing original manuscripts, nor do I possess the language skills to translate those manuscripts.

I would also like to mention that many of the purposes listed for the various Demons in the hierarchies and Demon directory come from a Christian viewpoint. The only way you can actually know a Demon's true attributes is to work with that Demon. The lessons a Demon can teach, or an attribute it has, can vary depending on what the practitioner needs and what wisdom the Demon can impart. For example, many people attribute Asmodeous to lust exclusively. I've successfully worked with him and sought his wisdom and guidance regarding physical therapy and exercise. He's proven to me to be quite adept in that area.

In other instances, some practitioners view Demons such as Lucifer and Leviathan in the feminine rather than the masculine. This is likely because each Demon has a balance.

So take the information on the following pages for what it's worth. Just remember to always follow your gut. Remember that Demons are never "evil", though some of their lessons for you may seem harsh. Sometimes that harshness is necessary when trying to get a point across. If you find yourself constantly having bad experiences with Demons or a specific Demon, chances are you are doing something wrong, or are missing the point of the lesson they are trying to impart.

# The Demonic Hierarchies

Demons have been catalogued since 100-400 A.D. This was around the time when the Testament of Solomon appeared, having described the magic ring for commanding the DJINN (i.e. Goetic Demons). The Djinn (also jinn) were originally genies from Arabic mythology who granted people wishes. Unfortunately, this particular idea of Demons has stuck with people.

Perhaps one of the most famous Demonologists is Johan Weyer who developed the most complex hierarchy known, consisting of over seven thousand Demons serving under seventy-two princes of hell. Unfortunately I only have Weyer's major Demons listed here. It is important to note that the Goetic hierarchy is the basis for many of these.

It is almost impossible to find all of these hierarchies in one publication. They are compiled from numerous sources including literature. The author of the Hierarchy is provided when known.

## From Collin De Plancy's Dictionaire Infernale (1863)

Asmodeus - The Destroyer
Astaroth - Obtains friendship of great lords.
Behemoth - Demon of indulgence
Ronwe - Demon of lingual knowledge
Urobach - Of the lower order of Demons
Andras - Grand Marquis of Hell, causes discord and quarrels
Beelzebub - Lord of the flies

## Sir William Fletcher Barrett's The Magus (1801)

Mammon - Prince of tempters
Asmodeus - Prince of vengeance
Satan - Prince of deluders
Belzebuth - Chief of false gods
Pytho - Prince of the spirits of deceit
Beliel - Prince of iniquity
Merihim - Prince of the spirits of pestilence
Abbadon - Prince of war
Astaroth - Prince of accusers and inquisitors

## From the Grimoire of Pope Honorius: (1600's)

### PRINCIPLE INFERNAL SPIRITS:
Lucifer - Emperor
Beelzebub - Prince
Astarot - Grand Duke

### SUPERIOR SPIRITS:
- Lucifage Rofocale - Prime Minister
- Satanchia - Grand General
- Agaliarept - Aussi General
- Feurety - Lieutenant Commander

- Sargantanas - Major
- Nebiros - Field Marshall

## SUBORDINATE SPIRITS
Bael , Bathim, Agares, Pursan, Marbas, Abigar, Pruslas, Loray, Aamon,Valefar, Barbatos, Forau, Buer, Ayperos, Gusoyn, Nuberus, Botis, Glasyabolis

## Johan Weyer's Hierarchy of Hell (1515-1588):
**(A. E. Waite?)** *Weyer, who studied under Cornelius Agrippa, is the very same 16th Century Demonologist John Weir (also spelt Wier at times) talked about in many freemasonry books. However, since the written record contains both Johan Weyer and John Weir and the hierarchy listings are slightly different, both have been included under separate entries.* **Please note:** A recent discussion with an occult scholar further suggests that this hierarchy is actually from *A.E. Waite*, who took liberties with Weyer's work, and the mistake of this hierarchy was repeated from Waite's work and placed in subsequent books as historical fact and attributed to Weyer. This particular hierarchy listing was extracted from such books. I am told this hierarchy does not appear in Weyer's **Pseudomonarchia Daemonum** and that Weyer's hierarchy is simply a revamp of the Goetia (as many are). See John Weir's hierarchy below for the hierarchy (and I believe that's a partial) that does come from Weyer's work.:

- Beelzebuth - Supreme Chieftain
- Satan - Occupies second place as prince of darkness.
- Eurynomous - Prince of death
- Moloch - Prince of the land of tears
- Pluto - Prince of fire
- Baal - Commander of the armies of hell
- Lucifer - Dispenses justice

- Asmodeus - Gambling
- Baalberith - Minister of pacts and treaties
- Proserpine - Prince of Demonic spirits
- Astaroth - Prince and treasurer of hell
- Nergal - Chief of secret police
- Bael - King, lord of the East, and commands 66 legions
- Forcas - President
- Beur - President and commands 50 legions
- Marchocias- Marquis and commands 30 legions
- Behamoth - unknown

Chamos, Melchom, Dagon, Adramalek

**John Weir's Hierarchy (partial):** *John Weir(Wier) is the same 16th Century Demonologist as Johan Weyer, student of Agrippa. However, since the written record contains both Johan Weyer and John Weir, and the hierarchy listings are somewhat different, both have been included under separate entries.* See Weyer above for more information about the possible misinformation of the above Weyer hierarchy.

-Bael - King, lord of the East, and commands 66 legions
-Forcas-President
-Beur - President and commands 50 legions
-Marchocias- Marquis and commands 30 legions
-Behamoth - unkown

**Sebastien Michaelis's Histoire admirable de la Possession et conversion d'une penitente (1613)**

**FIRST HIERARCHY**

Belzebuth - pride
Leviathan - faith
Asmodeus - luxury

Balberith - blasphemy and murder
Astaroth - vanity and sloth
Verrine - impatience
Gresil - impurity
Sonnillon - hate

## SECOND HIERARCHY

Carreau - mercilessness
Carnivean - obscenity
Oeillet - riches and wealth
Rosier - love
Verrier - disobedience

## THIRD HIERARCHY

Belial - arrogance
Olivier - cruelty and greed
Juvart - Demonic possession

## Peter Binsfeld's Demons of the Seven Deadly Sins (1589)

Lucifer - pride
Mammon - avarice
Asmodeus - lechery
Satan - anger
Beelzebub - gluttony
Leviathan - envy
Belphegore - sloth

## Faust's Hierarchy of the Kingdoms:

Beelzebub - North
Lucifer - East
Belial - South
Astaroth - West

Phlegathon - Center (Not an actual Demon, but a river. Phlegathon means center in Greek.)

## *Misc. Medieval Hierarchies of Unknown Origin*
Possibly from the obscure Liber Perditionis; a medieval book of Demons and their rank in the infernal hierarchy.

## THE SEVEN PRINCES OF HELL

Baal-beryth - master of rituals and pacts
Dumah - commander of the Demons of gehEnna
Meririm - prince of air
Rahab - prince of oceans
Sariel - Prince of the moon
Mephistopholes - the destroyer
Lucifer Rofocale - prime minister and controls wealth

## ARCH DEMONS OF HELL

Adramaleck - Prince of Fire
Carniveau - Demon of Possession
Python - Prince of lying spirits
Mammon - Prince of tempters, avarice, and greed
Rimmon - Prince of lightning and storms

## ARCH SHE-DEMONS

Leviathan - The Chaos Dragon
Barbelo - Unknown
Proserpine - Destroyer
Astarte - Queen of spirits of the dead
Agrat-bat-mahlaht - One of Satan's wives and Demoness of whores
Eisheth Zenunim - Same as above
Lilith - Satan's favorite wife
Naamah - Demoness of seduction

**The Goetic Hierarchy**

Listed in Traditional Order as such: Name, Element, and Several Correspondences.

1. **Bael** – Fire, espionage.
2. **Agares** – Earth, communication and reconciliation.
3. **Vassago** – Water, divination.
4. **Samigina** (also Gamigin) – Water, necromancy, uncovering secrets, corrections, and sciences.
5. **Marbas** - Air, transformation.
6. **Valefor** – Earth, familiars and recovering lost items.
7. **Amon** - Water, material and mundane matters as well as relationships.
8. **Barbatos** – Fire, favors, insight into reality, and communication with animals.
9. **Paimon** – Water, charisma, binding, honor, and art.
10. **Buer** - Fire, healing and herbalism.
11. **Gusion** – Water, divination, honor, and dignity.
12. **Sitri** – Earth, sexual desire and attraction.
13. **Beleth** – Earth, sexual passion.
14. **Leraje** (also Leraikha)- Fire, overcoming obstacles, competition (winning) as well as corruption.
15. **Eligos** – Water, practical strategy.
16. **Zepar** – Earth, infertility.
17. **Botis** – Water, reconciliation.
18. **Bathin** - Earth, transformation and travel both physical and spiritual.
19. **Sallos** (also Saleos) Earth, love.
20. **Purson** – Earth, assistance and favor.
21. **Marax** (also Narax) Earth, wisdom.
22. **Ipos** – Water, courage through presence and grace.
23. **Aim** – Fire, victory through activity.
24. **Naberius** – Air, the bridge between this world and the spirit world.

25. **Glasya-Labolas** – Fire, for commanding the conclusion of something.
26. **Bune** (also Bime) – Earth, spiritual protection and wealth.
27. **Ronove** – Air, gain through charm and charisma.
28. **Berith** – Fire, for status of honor, power and respect.
29. **Astaroth** – Earth, psychic protection and success.
30. **Forneus** – Water, recognition through fame and fortune.
31. **Foras** – Earth, wisdom, stamina, and understanding.
32. **Asmoday** – Air, intelligence and skill.
33. **Gaap** – Air, ignorance and astral travel.
34. **Furfur** – Fire, transformation, attraction, and aggressive behavior.
35. **Marchosias** – Fire, strength and prosperity.
36. **Stolas** (also Stolos)– Air, clarity of mind and practicality in all matters.
37. **Phenex** (also Pheynix)– Air, harmony and art.
38. **Halphas** – Fire, ambition and power.
39. **Malphas**– Air, strength and aspirations.
40. **Raum** – Fire, justice.
41. **Focalor** – Water, failure and reversing curses.
42. **Vepar** – Water, balance of karma and destruction.
43. **Sabnock** – Fire, construction and victory.
44. **Shax** – Air, immobility and confusion.
45. **Vine** – Water, exposure of negative influences and psychic protection.
46. **Bifrons** – Earth, memory and spiritual communication.
47. **Uvall** (also Vual or Voval)– Water, sensuality, luxury, history and the finer things in life.
48. **Haagenti** – Earth, alchemy, transformation and change.
49. **Crocell** – Water, instinct, intuition, and pleasure.
50. **Furcas** – Air, divination and psychic power.
51. **Balam** – Earth, revelation and the ability to uncover hidden thngs.

52. **Alloces** – Fire, spiritual understanding and wisdom. Attracting familiars.
53. **Camio** (also Caim) – Air, intuition and diplomacy in business affairs.
54. **Murmur** (also Murmus)- Water, learning and spiritual communication.
55. **Orobas** – Water, influence for fame and recognition.
56. **Gremory** (also Gemory or Gamori) – Water, gain in all areas of life including love and wealth.
57. **Ose** (also Voso or Oso) – Air, answers secrets and transformation.
58. **Amy** (also Avnas) – Fire, treasures, knowledge, and astrology.
59. **Oriax** (also Orias) – Air, prediction, honors, and astrology.
60. **Vapula** (also Naphula) – Air, endeavors of expertise, knowledge, philosophy and sciences.
61. Zagan – Earth, transmutation, wisdom, and wealth.
62. **Volac** (also Valak, Valac, or Valu)– Earth, discovery of treasure and/or hidden enemies.
63. **Andras** – Fire, to overthrow enemies and create or dispel discord.
64. **Haures** (also Flauros, Haurus, or Havres) – Fire, new beginnings, justice, and balance.
65. **Andrealphus** - Air, measurement, foresight, and transformation.
66. **Cimejes** (also Cimeies or Kimaris) – Earth, strength and structure.
67. **Amdusias** (also Amdukias)– Air, music and manipulation.
68. **Belial** – Fire, mastery, political power, dignities, and favors.
69. **Decarabia** – Air, visions and illusions.
70. **Seere** (also Sear or Seir)- Air, action, putting things into motion and discovering thieves.
71. **Dantalion** – Water, persuasion, telepathy, and visions.

72. **Andromalius** – Fire, retribution and justice.

## [1]Richard Dukanté's Hierarchy (1963)

- Satan - King
- Unsere - Fertility and Sorcery
- Satanchia - Grand General (War)
- Agaliarept - Assistant Grand General (War)
- Lucifage - High Command (Control)
- Flereous - Fire Elemental
- Lucifer - Air Elemental
- Leviathan - Water Elemental
- Belial - Earth Elemental
- Beelzebuth - Lord of insects
- Belphegore - Master of Armorment and Weaponry
- Mesphito - Keeper of the book of death
- Amducious - The destroyer
- Asmodeus - Demon of Lust
- Sonnilion - Demoness of hate
- Abbadon - Advisor
- Ammon - Demon of domination
- Mammon - Demon of Avarice
- Rosier - Demon of love
- Ashtaroth - Priestess of friendship
- Eurynomous - Demon of Death
- Verrine - Demon of Health
- Ronwe - Demon of Knowledge
- Babeal - Keeper of Graves

---

[1] Printed here with the permission of Selinda T. Dukanté.

**The Demonic Aspects** - the true Hierarchy of Richard Dukanté.

The hierarchy is composed of nine different families including 39 infernal hierarchs of note:

## Family 1
- Satan - King
- Unsere - Fertility and Sorcery
- Satanchia - Grand General (War)
- Agaliarept - Assistant Grand General (War)
- Lucifage - High Command (Control)
- Flereous - Fire Elemental
- Lucifer - Air Elemental
- Beelzebuth - Lord of insects
- Belphegore - Master of Armorment and Weaponry-gain
- Mesphito - Keeper of the book of death
- Delepitoré- Demoness of magick.
- Belial - Earth Elemental

## Family 2
- Luithian - Advisor
- Leviathan - Water Elemental
- Sonnelion - Demoness of hate

## Family 3
- Abbadon - Advisor
- Ammon - Demon of domination
- Mammon - Demon of Avarice

## Family 4
- Rosier - Demon of love
- Astarte - Demoness of love
- Ashtaroth - Priestess of friendship

- Astarot - Matters concerning the heart
- Amducious - The destroyer
- Asmodeus - Demon of Lust

## Family 5
- Eurynomous - Demon of Death
- Balberith - Prince of dying
- Babeal - Keeper of Graves

## Family 6
- Verrine - Demon of Health
- Verrier - Demoness of herbal knowledge
- Ronwe - Demon of Knowledge

## Family 7
- Svengali - Demon of Vengeance
- Tezrian - Priestess of battle

## Family 8
- Asafoetida - Demoness of feminine attributes
- Rashoon - Priestess of seduction
- Taroon - Priestess of Desire

## Family 9

Consists of lesser hierarchy


## The Nine Demonic Divinities[2]

Satan - He through which all energy flows
Lucifer - air

---

[2] The nine Demonic divinities first appeared in 1312 in the Black Book of Thoman Buchan according to the Delaney Family Grimoire.

Flereous - fire
Leviathan - water
Belial - earth
Amducious - negative polarity
Verrine - positive polarity
Unsere - life
Eurynomous - death

# Creating Personal Pantheons

Many Demonolators find that an existing pantheon works just fine. We like the familiar. If you're comfortable with the pantheon you're currently working with then you have no reason to change it. Leave it be. This section is for those Demonolators who find they aren't really connecting with an existing pantheon.

In this case, a personal pantheon can be the solution for the Demonolator who doesn't feel comfortable working with any of the defined pantheons out there.

For some people simple labels for Demons of a pantheon work just fine. Others, however, prefer their external energy sources to be named. For the Satanist, Satan, Lucifer, Set, Belial or a whole host of Demon names may point to the same source of energy. Or they may be separate.

The point being that you should choose the labels or names of Demons that you feel you have a personal relationship with. Your next question might be, "How does one go about finding out which god-forms one has a personal relationship with?"

I always like to suggest that people meditate on Demons first to get a feel for them. Meditate on the names and any corresponding representations you can find. You will quickly find that there are some Demons you do not feel connected to while others you feel a deep bond with. Once you've chosen those Demons you are most comfortable with – work with them. Nothing will be more telling than how you and the Demon work together. Keep a journal of these exercises then go back through your notes. Which Demons were most effective? Which of them seemed to be a strong part of yourself? Most importantly, was there a connection? Like with a good friend, you will immediately *click* with a Demon compatible with you.

*Note that this is also a great exercise to do when you're looking to find your matron/patron.*

For those who wish to create a personal pantheon, make a list of the Demons you feel most drawn to and connected with. Once you have done the mediations and workings like the ones mentioned above, choose those that you felt the strongest connections with. I've been told by many people that the Demon they one time felt most connected to changes as life situations and experiences changed the individual.

**Organizing Your Pantheon**

If your pantheon is simple such as you have one Demon for each earth, air, fire, water, spirit – then organization may not be important. However, if you find yourself with an ever-growing list of compatible Demons, you may choose to organize them for your own personal use.

Organizing the pantheon can be tackled in one of several ways. You can list them by time of year you feel most connected, you can sort them by day and night, you can sort them by color, element, emotion, purpose, or even alphabetically. These are just a few ideas for those Demonolators who like to list and categorize because they enjoy being organized.

**Working With Your Pantheon**

The more you work with your personal pantheon, the more acquainted you will become with each individual Demon. I think we all tend to have a short list of those Demons we become closest to. You may discover you have given them a form and appearance unique to your vision. You may discover their strengths and flaws. You will undoubtedly realize that each Demon has its own *personality*. This is perfectly normal (you're not nuts) and it's okay. Oftentimes Demons take on the role of altar ego – things we wish we were. Allow this to happen because it is through these sources that we can discover ourselves, and the hidden potential we have. A Demon who takes on the role of altar ego can help us be less shy, or to stand up for ourselves.

There is only one way you can work with your own pantheon. And that's by following your own gut and working with them in a manner that feels right and comfortable for you. If that means you give offerings of pumpkins and gourds to your Demonic earth element every autumn – so be it!

Far too often in the occult and alternative religion world we judge what is the right and wrong way to work with our Demonic pantheons based on grimoires and guides written by other people who made up the rules. If you are comfortable with their rules (and there will be others' rules you'll like) then make them your own.

Otherwise, create your own rules. Of course it's advisable to make sure your personal rules are ethical, moral, and do not break the laws of your state or country. We still must conform to societal law, especially when the reputations of our fellow brethren are judged on the behavior of each of us. This means that you should not practice physical sacrifices of humans or non-food animals (I've never met a Demon who asked me to kill anyone!) nor steal, nor rape, etc... I have never met a Demon who demands any of these things, nor have I met any serious and mentally stable Demonolators who have done any of these things. We'd like to keep it that way.

Of course feel free to curse the hell out of anyone who seriously wrongs you. Feel free to practice sex magick with willing, legal-aged partners (use safe sex always!), practice masturbation during ritual, and use drops of your own blood during ritual. All of these things are traditional within the realm of Demonolatry practice and are **not** considered morally bad or ethically questionable by most Demonolators. I say *most* because each individual has personal boundaries.

What I mean by following your gut is something like as follows: For me, Belial doesn't care for food as an offering. He (he's a he to me) prefers mulch and dirt. For others, fresh produce is the only offering fit for an earth Demon. In reality, who's to say if He cares for either? Or perhaps the earth Demons like it all. All I can know for certain is what feels right to me. All you can know for certain is what feels right for you. That is the premise behind the personal pantheon. You do not have to limit yourself to Demons of the Christian or Demonolatry pantheons. You can also look to Egyptian, Roman, and Greek pantheons if you feel they suit you.

# The Demon Directory[3]

This is by no means a complete listing of every Demon in existence. To compile something as complete would be a lifetime task since there are millions of Demons spanning our world's diverse cultures. Nor is this directory meant to give complete information on each Demon listed. This is merely a quick reference supplied so that Demonolators might better understand the human attributed functions of each Demon in its perspective role within history, religion, and mythology. Much of this is from a Christian viewpoint. Please keep this in mind when choosing a Demon to work with. Always remember that the best way to figure out what a Demon can offer is to work with the Demon itself because sometimes their purpose is unique to the individual.

---

[3] This directory first published by S. Connolly electronically at Tezrian's Vault Demonolatry www.Demonolatry.com

# A

**Abaddon** - (Hebrew) Destroyer, Advisor. Said to be chief of Demons. Sometimes regarded as the destroying angel.

**Abdiel**- (Arabic) from "Abd" meaning slave. Lord of slaves/slavery.

**Abduxuel** - (Enochian) One of the Demonic rulers of the lunar mansions.

**Abigor** - (Unk) allegedly a warrior Demon who commands sixty legions. Weyer names him as god of Grand Duke of Hell. Appears in a pleasant form. Also Abigar - Can foretell future and give military advice.

**Aclahayr**- (Unk) Of the fourth hour of the Nuctemeron, the genius spirit.

**Adad**, Addu- (Babylonian, Hittite) god of the storm.

**Adramalech** - (Samarian) devil. Commander of Hell. Wierius' chancellor of infernal regions. In Assyria where he was worshipped, children were supposedly burned at his altars.

**Adriel** - Mansions of the moon among the Enochian Demons.

**Aeshma**, **Aesma**- (Persian) One of seven archangels of the Persians. Adopted later into Hebrew mythology as Asmodeus. Has been recorded in history for at least three thousand years. Said to be a small hairy Demon able to make men perform cruel acts.

**Ahazu-Demon** - the seizure Demon of the night.

**Agaliarept** - (Hebrew) commander of armies. Aussi General of hell - Grimoire of Pope Honorius..

**Agares** or Aguares- (Unk) devil. Wierius' hierarchy states Agares is the Demon of courage.

**AgathoDemon** - (Egyptian) a good Demon worshipped by the Egyptians.

**Agramon** - (Unk) Demon of fear

**Agrat-bat-mahlaht** - One of Satan's wives and Demoness of whores.

**Ahpuch** - (Mayan) devil.

**Ahriman** - (Mazdean) devil. Ahremanes was the name given to fallen angels by the Persians.

**Alastor** - (Unk) Wierius' cruel Demon called "the executioner."

**Aldinach** - (Egyptian) A Demon who causes natural disasters (i.e. floods, hurricanes, tornadoes, earthquakes).

**Allocen**- One of the 72 spirits of Solomon.

**Alocer, Allocer**- (Unk) Grand duke of hell. One of Solomon's 72 spirits.

**Alu-Demon** - (Semitic) Night Demon.

**Amaimon**- One of the 72 spirits of Solomon.

**Amaymon** - Evil Spirit, king of South.

**Amducious** - (Hebrew) The destroyer. Also Amducias - Grand Duke of Hades. According to Wierius a Demon of music.

**Amon, Ammon** - (Egyptian) Sun God. Much like Lucifer except controls reproduction and life. See also Amaimon, Amoymon, Amaymon, and Aamon.

**Amy** - One of the 72 spirits of Solomon. Said to be supreme president of hell. He will trade knowledge for the human soul.

**Anamelech, Anomylech** - (Assyrian) bearer of bad news. An obscure Demon. His name means "good king". Some sources claim Anamelech is the moon goddess while Andramalech is the sun god.

**Andras** - (Unk) god of quarrels. Grand marquis of hell.

**Andrealphus** - One of the 72 Spirits of Solomon.

**Andromalius**- One of the 72 Spirits of Solomon.

**Anini** - One of the 72 Spirits of Solomon.

**Anneberg** - (German) Demon of mines.

**Ansitif** - (unk) Possessed Sister Barbara of St. Michael in 1643 during the possessions of the nuns at Louviers.

**Apollyn** - (Greek) Another name for Satan.

**Ardat-Lile** - (Semitic) a female spirit/Demon who weds human beings and wreaks havoc in the dwellings of men.

**Arioch** - (unk) Demon of vengeance. He delivers vengeance only when called on.

**Arphaxat** - (Unk) The Demon who possessed Loise de Pinterville during the possession of the nuns at Loudun.

**Ashtaroth**, **Astaroth** (Phonician)- goddess of lust, seduction. Same as Ishtar. Turned male in Christian mythology - Lord Treasurer of Hell. Prince of accusers and inquisitors. Demon of vanity and sloth. One of the 72 spirits of Solomon.

**Asmodeus**, **Asmoday** - (Hebrew) god of lust. A Demon most commonly involved in possession cases, particularly noted in the possession of the Louviers nuns. Evolved from the Persian Aeshma. See Aeshma.

**Astarte**- Queen of spirits of the dead.

**Aym** - (Unk) Grand duke of hell. Also Haborym.

**Ayperos**- (Unk) Prince of hell. Subordinate in Grimoire of Pope Honorius.

**Azazel** - (Hebrew) god/Demon of war. See also Azael.

# B

**Baal**, **Bael** (Hebrew) devil. Means "the lord." The Canaanites worshipped Baal and held rituals at which children were burned for sacrifice. According to Wierius, this Demon is the first monarch of hell and appears as a three headed beast. Bael is cited in the Grand Grimiore as commanding general of infernal armies.

**Baalberith**, **Balberith** - (Canaanite) Lord of covenant later made god of death. According to Wierius - a Demon master of the infernal alliance. In some hierarchies he is the secretary of the archives of hell. Demon of blasphemy and murder.

**Baalzephon** - (Canaanite) Captain of guard and sentinels of Hell according to Wierius.

**Babael** - (Unk) Keeper of graves.

**Balaam** - (Hebrew) avarice and greed.

**Balan** - (Unk) A Demon in Wierius' hierarchy said to be high in the monarchy. The Demon of finesse and ruses. Also a prince of hell.

**Balban** - (Unk) a Demon of delusion.

**Baltazo**- (Unk)The Demon who possessed Nicole Aubry of Laon in 1566.

**Baphomet** - God of the Templars. Worshiped as Satan. The Knight's Templar are thought, by some, to be one of the earliest sects of Demonolatry.

**Barbas**- (Unk) a Demon of mechanics according to some hierarchies.

**Barbetos**- (Unk) Duke of Hades.

**Bar-Lgura** - (Semitic) A gargoyle type Demon who is said to sit atop houses and pounce on the inhabitants.

**Barqu** -(Unk) The Demon who keeps the secrets of the philosophers stone.

**Barzabel** - Associated with Machidael and Barchiel.

**Bast** -(Egyptian) goddess of pleasure. Represented by a cat.

**Bathym, Bathim, Bathin**- (Unk) See also Marthim. Demon of herbs and precious stones according to Wierius. One of the 72 spirits of Solomon.

**Bayemon** - (Unk) According to the Grimiore of Pope Honorius a reigning monarch Demon presiding over western infernal region.

**Bechard**, Bechaud- (Unk) A Demon mentioned in Key Of Solomon as Demon of tempests. Demon of the natural forces.

**Beelzebub, Beelzebuth, Belzebath**- (Hebrew) Lord of Flies. Among the Demons blamed for the Demonic possessions of the nuns at Loudun. Chief of false gods.

**Behemoth** - (Hebrew) Another name for Satan.

**Beherit** - (Syriac) Another name for Satan.

**Belial** or Beliar- (Hebrew) The earth elemental. Speculation has suggested the name Belial comes from the Hebrew phrase beli ya 'al meaning "without worth." Prince of trickery. One of the 72 princes of Solomon.

**Belphegor, Belphegore, Baalphegor**- (Moabites) Demon of discovery, invention, and riches.

**Berith** - One of the 72 Spirits of Solomon.

**Biffant** - (Unk) The Demon who allegedly possessed Denise de la Caille.

**Bifrons** - (Unk) Wierius' Demon of astronomy, geometry, and other such sciences. A Demon who lights strange lights above tombs of the dead.

**Bile'** - (Celtic) god of Hell.

**Bileth** - One of the 72 Spirits of Solomon.

**Blisargon** - (Unk) Grand enticer of thieves until he brings his followers to destruction.

**Botis** - One of the 72 spirits of Solomon.

**Buer**- (Unk) a Demon of the second order who commands fifty legions. One of the 72 Spirits of Solomon.

**Bune** - (Unk) One of Wierius' Demons of death.

# C

**Caacrinolaas** - (Unk) Wierius' Demon of knowledge of liberal arts. Appears as a Griffon. Also Grand President of Hell. Also Caasimolar or Glasya.

**Cambions** - (Unk) Offspring of Incubi and Succubi.

**Carreau** - Mercilessness.

**Cassiel, Caspiel**- (Unk) Ruler of Saturn.

**Caym, Caim** - (Unk) Grand President of Hell. One of the 72 Spirits of Solomon.

**Chamos** - no description.

**Charon** - Boatman of hell. Ferries souls across styx and/or archeron. From Dante's Inferno.

**Chax** - (Unk) Grand duke of hell. Also Scox.

**Chemosh** - (Moabite) devil.

**Chomie** - (Enochian) no description.

**Cimeries** - (African) devil.

**Clauneck** - Demon over treasures and riches.

**Clisthert**- (Unk) a Demon who can change day to night and night to day.

**Colopatiron** - Of the 9th hour of the Nuctemeron, genius. Sets prisons open.

**Cresil** - (Unk) Demon of impurity and slovenliness. Also Gressil.

**Cunali** - One of the Demons of the 8th hour of the Nuctemeron.

**Cusion** - no description.

# D

**Dagon** - (Philistine) another serpent god and god of ocean.

**Dabriel** - no description

**Dameal**, **Deamiel**- no description

**Dantalian** - One of the 72 Spirits of Solomon.

**Decarabia** - One of the 72 Spirits of Solomon.

**Delepitorae**, **Delepitoré**- (Unk) Demoness of sorcery enlightenment.

**Demogorgon**, **Gorgo** - (Greek) devil.

**Demoriel** - no description

**Diriel** - no description

**Dracula** - (Romanian) devil.

# E

**Eblis** - (Mohammedan) god of fire. Also Haris.

**Emma-O** - (Japanese) ruler of Hell.

**Euronymous**, **Eurynomous** - (Greek) god of death. Prince of hell who feeds upon corpses.

# F

**Flereous**, **Feurety** - (Unk) god of fire. Fire Elemental used in place of Satan. Lieutenant of hell.

**Furfur** - (Unk) Holds rank as count of hell.

# G

**Geryon** - (literary- Dante) Centaur/Dragon who guards hell.

**Guecubu** - (Chili) Evil spirits.

# H

**Haborym** - (Hebrew) Another name for Satan.

**Hecate** - (Greek) goddess of underworld and sorcery. Queen of witches.

**Hela** - (Teutonic) goddess of death, daughter of Loki.

# I

**Ifrits** - (Arabic) Evil, hideous spectres. Became Genies in Persian and Indian mythology. Also associated with Jinns and Divs of Persia.

**Incubus** - male Demon of seduction said to invade a woman's dreams. Note various spellings: Inncubus, Inccubus. Plural = Incubi

**Ishtar** - (Babylonian) goddess of fertility.

# J

**Jezebeth** - (Unk) the Demon of falsehoods.

# K

**Kali** - (Hindu) daughter of Shiva, the destroyer. A succubus/succumbus.

**Kasdeya** - The book of enoch refers to this Demon as the "fifth satan"

**Kobal** - (Unk) Hell's entertainment liaison.

**Kostchtchie** - (Russian) a goblin of death.

# L

**Leonard** - (see also Urian; German) Demon of sorcery . Appears as a giant black goat.

**Leviathan** - (Hebrew) the serpent, the raging sea. Snake worship. Water Elemental. Grand admiral of hell. Seen as androgynous.

**Lilith** - (Hebrew) in Hebrew myth - Adam's first wife. Later wife to Satan. According to many Demonologists, Lilith presides over Succubi. Lilith is said to attempt to destroy newborn infants. For this reason the practice of writing a formula to drive Lilith away on all four corners of the birth chamber was adopted by the Jews. Lilith is the princess of hell.

**Loki** - (Teutonic) devil.

**Lucifer** - (Roman) The Light Bringer. Air Elemental. Often misconstrued as being Satan. They are two separate Demons.

**Lucifuge**, **Lucifuge Rofocale** - (Roman) devil.

# M

**Malphas** - (Unk) Grand president of the infernal regions. Appears as a crow.

**Mammon** - (Aramaic) god of wealth & profit.

**Mandragoras** - (Unk) Familiar Demons. They are attributed to the mandrake root and considered gifts from Satan to the sorcerer who conjures them.

**Mania** - (Etruscan) goddess of Hell.

**Mantus** - (Etruscan) god of hell.

**Mara** - (Buddhist) a Demon who attempts to damn the soul.

**Mastema** - (Unk) leader of human/Demon offspring

**Melchom** - (Unk) the treasurer of the palace of hell.

**Mephistopholes**, **Mesphito** - (Greek) the light shunner. Counterpart of Lucifer.

**Merihim** - (unk) the prince of pestilence.

**Metztli** - (Aztec) goddess of night

**Mictain** -(Aztec) god of death

**Moloch** - (Phoenician) devil

**Mormo** - (Greek) God of Spirits. Hecate's Consort.

**Mullin** - (Unk) Leonard's right hand man.

**Murmur**- (Unk) Demon of music. A count of hell.

# N
**Naamah** - (Hebrew) seduction

**Naburus, Naberios** - (Unk) protector of the gates of hell. Associated with Cerberos. A marquis of hell.

**Nebiros** - (Unk) Mar De Camp of hell.

**Nergal** - (Babylonian) god of underworld. A second order Demon.

**Nihasa** - (American Indian) devil.

**Nija** - (Polish) god of underworld

**Nina** -(Babylonian) Serpent Goddess.

**Nybras** - (Unk) an inferior Demon who publicizes the pleasures of hell.

**Nysrogh**- (Unk) another second order Demon - who- is chief of staff in the palace of hell.

# O

**Orias** - (Unk) Demon of divination. Marquis of hell.

**Oroan** - (Guyana) Demon of the eclipse.

**Orthon** - (Unk) a Demon of unknown origin who is said to have ties with possessions in France and with the Satanic-Masonic cult of Palladinism in 19th century Italy.

**O'Yama** - (Japanese) Another name for Satan.

# P

**Pan** - (Greek) god of lust.

**Paymon** - (Unk) master of infernal ceremonies.

**Philotanus** - (Unk) a second order Demon in service to Belial.

**Pluto** - (Roman) god of underworld.

**Proserpine** - (Greek) queen of underworld.

**Pwcca** - (Welsh) Pooka in Celtic Mythos derived from this name for Satan.

**Pyro** - (Unk) A Demon prince of falsehood.

**Pytho** - (Unk) a Demon of lies. A serpent Demon.

# Q

# R

**Rahu** - (Hindu) devil.

**Rakshasa** - (India) Demon whose appearance in the least, horrifying.

**Raum**- (Unk) a count of hell.

**Rimmon** - (Syrian) devil.

**Ronwe** - (Unk) the Demon of knowledge. In some accounts - a lesser Demon.

# S

**Sabazios** - (Phrygian) the snake. Serpent worship.

**Samael** - (Unk) it is thought this angel of death was the Demon who tempted Eve. Also the prince of air. This is merely another name for satan.

**Samnu** - (Asian) devil.

**Satan**, Shaitan (Satan/Hebrew Shaitan/Arabic) The Adversary. Lord of fire. Fire Elemental.

**Satanchia** (Hebrew/Greek) devil. Same as Satan.

**Sargatanas** - brigadier of hell.

**Sedit** (American Indian) devil.

**Sekhmet** (Egyptian) goddess of vengeance.

**Semiazas** - (Unk) said to be the chief of all fallen angels.

**Set** - (Egyptian) devil.

**Shabriri** - (Jewish Myth) a Demon who strikes people blind.

**Shiva** - (Hindu) the destroyer.

**Sonnilion**, Sonnillon - (Armenian) goddess of hate.

**Succorbenoth** - (Unk) Demon of jealousy and said to protect gates and bridgeways.

**Succumbus, Succubus**- female Demon of seduction. Said to seduce males while sleeping. Note various spellings. Plural - Succubi.

**Supay** - (Inca) god of underworld.

# T

**T'an-mo** - (Chinese) devil of desire.

**Tchort** - (Russian) The Black God. Another name for Satan.

**Tezcatlipoca** - (Aztec) god of Hell.

**Tezrian** - (Armenian) goddess of war

**Thamuz** - (Sumerian) devil. An ambassador of hell. Said to have started the inquisition and to have invented artillary.

**Thoth** - (Egyptian) god of magick.

**Troian** - (Russian) night Demon.

**Tunrida** - (Scandanavian) devil.

**Typhon** - (Greek) Another name for Satan.

# U

**Ukobach** or **Urobach** - (Unk) a fire Demon.

**Unsere** - (Unk) goddess of sorcery and fertility.

**Uphir** - (Unk) the head Demon physician in the palace of hell.

# V

**Valafar**- (unk) another grand duke of hell.

**Veltis** - (Babylonian) Evil spirit who assaulted St. Margaret.

**Verdelet** - (Unk) Master of ceremonies of infernal court. Demon of the second order.

**Verin** also **Verrine** and **Verraine**- (Unk) the Demon of impatience.

**Vetis** - (Unk) the temptor of the holy.

# W

# X

**Xaphan** - (Unk) another fire Demon. Keeper of the furnaces of hell.

# Y

**Yaotzin** - (Aztec) god of Hell.

**Yen-lo-Wang** (Chinese) ruler of Hell.

# Z

**Zabulon** - (Unk) Demon who possessed one of the nuns at Loudun.

**Zaebos** - (Sumerian) Grand Count of hell said to have gentile disposition.

**Zagam** - (Unk) Grand king and president of infernal regions. Said to change things into its opposite. Demon of counterfeit.

**Zapan** - (Unk) One of the kings of hell according to Wierius.

**Zeernebooch**- (German) monarch of the empire of the dead.

**Zepar** - (Unk) Grand duke of hell - god of war. Also Vepar and Separ

# Demons Based On Purpose

This is simply a quick reference to find Demons fast. It's handy when you want to do a ritual working for one of the following reasons and want to consider all of your options. Not every Demon is here, nor is every purpose. This list is based on the most common purposes people might perform rites for.

### Love -- Lust -- Relationships -- Compassion

Rosier
Astarte
Ashtaroth
Astaroth
Asmodeous
Agrat-bat-mahlaht
Eisheth-Zenunim
Lilith
Naamah
Asafoetida

Rashoone
Taroone

## Hatrid -- Vengence -- Anger -- War

Amducious
Andras
Merihim
Abbadon
Satanchia
Lucifuge-Rofocale
Agaliarept
Feurety
Sargatanas
Nebiros
Baal
Sonnilion
Tezrian
Olivier
Mephestophiles
Dumah
Proserpine
Belphegore
Svengali

## Life-Healing

Unsere
Verrine
Verrier
Belial

## Death

Eurynomous
Baalberith
Babael

## Nature

Belial
Lucifer
Satan
Flereous
Leviathan
Rimmon
Dagon
Rahab
Seriel

## Money-Prosperity-Luck

Behemoth
Belphegore
Asmodeous
Astaroth
Oeillet
Olivier
Beelzebub
Mammon

## Knowledge-Secrets-Sorcery

Ronwe
Pytho
Lucifer
Leviathan
Baalberith

Unsere
Delepitorae
Mesphito
Luithian
Abbadon
Verrier

# The Dukante Hierarchy

This particular section includes the Dukante Hierarchy and the Enns. Along with that, you will find notes from noted family grimoires and other Demonolators that discuss additional breakdowns, and additional information about these Demons including their descriptions. Please note the Enns (invocations) are underlined and italicized. More about the Enns will be discussed later in this book. Also note that the Dukante hierarchy is admittedly incomplete. Mr. Dukante died before he finished his work.

## Family 1

- Satan - King : *Tasa reme laris Satan - Ave Satanis* - Direction: Center/All ; Color: All ; Months: All ; Seasons All ; Rituals- Any.; Satan appears as a sage wise man with silver hair and black eyes. His eyes have been described as nothing and all.
- Unsere - (Female) Fertility and Sorcery: *Unsere tasa lirach on ca ayar* - Direction: Northeast;

Colors: Green and White; Month: February; Season: Late Winter; Ritual: Wisdom, patience, motherhood.; Unsere has deep green eyes like the fertile plains of Ireland [Editor's note - I saw her with blue eyes]. Her hair is brown with strands of spun silver. Her eyes smile and sparkle. Her energy is gentle and nurturing. She travels often in a cowl-hooded cloak. Most memorable are her thin, delicate, pale hands. She dissolves as a mist. She is said to often appear to women during or after childbirth to breath life into infants. [Delaney Grimoire Reference]

- Satanchia - Grand General (War) : *Furca na alle laris Satanchia* See information about the **Commanders**.
- Agaliarept - Assistant Grand General (War) : *On ca Agaliarept agna* - See information about the **Commanders**.
- Lucifage - High Command (Control) : *Eyen tasa valocur Lucifuge Rofocale* His twin brother is Lucifer. See information about the **Commanders**.
- Flereous - Fire Elemental : *Ganic Tasa Fubin Flereous* - Direction: South; Color: Red, Orange; Month: June; Season: Summer; Ritual: Baptism, action, love, solstice. Flereous appears as a tall man with long, red, course hair and red eyes. His voice is low and hissing. His expression is that of placidity. See information about **Elementals**.
- Lucifer - Air Elemental : *Renich Tasa Uberaca Biasa Icar Lucifer* - Direction: East; Colors: White Yellow; Month: March; Season: Spring; Ritual: Enlightenment, spring equinox, initiations. Lucifer appears with long, black hair and blue eyes. His voice is considered average though he seems overly excited most of the time. He wears pendants of

eagles. Twin to Lucifuge. See information about **Elementals**

- Beelzebuth - Lord of insects. [Editor's note - more recent translations of older texts say Beelzebuth was translated improperly and it should have been Lord of Lords. It is possible Dukante did not know this?] : *Adey vocar avage Beelzebuth*

- Belphegore - Master of Weaponry- gain: *Lyan Ramec Catya Ganen Belphegore*

- Mesphito - Keeper of the book of death: *Mesphito ramec viasa on ca*

- Delepitoré- (Female) Demoness of magick. : *Deyen pretore ramec Delepitore on ca* - She is tall and slender with blue/gray eyes. She possesses all knowledge of sorcery and carries with her an oak wand with a tip made of glazed crystal. She appears most often in blue robes and cloaks. Patient and reserved. Heed well to not anger her for she knows well the Demoness' Tezrian and Sonnellion.

- Belial - Earth Elemental: *Lirach Tasa Vefa Wehlc Belial* - Direction: North; Colors: Green, Brown, Black; Month: December; Season: Winter; Ritual: initiation, new beginnings, winter solstice. Belial appears with hair colored black and white like salt and pepper (some people report his hair to be blonde). His eyes shift from brown to green. His voice comes off as being quite normal, though he speaks with resolute confidence in everything he says. He often seems perplexed or confused by some great mystery. He is not as tall as some of the other elementals. See information about **Elementals**

## Family 2

- Luithian - Advisor: *Deyan anay tasa Luithian*

- *Azlyn - (Female) Weaves the threads of things to come, future. [New addition stemming from ascension 4/8/01] Her Enn was also begotten through ascension. *Rean Par Tasa Azlyn Ayar*
- Leviathan - Water Elemental: *Jaden Tasa Hoet Naca Leviathan* - Direction: West; Colors: Blue, Gray; Month: September; Season: Autumn; Ritual: emotions, initiation, equinox, healing, fertility. Leviathan appears with long black hair and blue/gray eyes so striking it is as if you are staring into the waters of your own soul. His voice is low, his speech reserved. He is also shorter than Lucifer and Flereous, but stands a hair taller than Belial. He wears an amulet of his own sigil. See information about **Elementals**
- Sonnelion - (Female) Demoness of hate: *Ayer Serpente Sonnillion* - Direction: Southwest; Colors: violet; Month: July; Season: Mid-summer; Ritual: dispersing anger, cursing, balancing, focus.

## Family 3

- Abbadon - Advisor: *Es na ayer Abbadon avage*
- Ammon - Demon of domination: *Avage Secore Ammon ninan* Twin to Mammon.
- Mammon - Demon of Avarice: *Tasa Mammon on ca lirach* Twin to Ammon.

**Family 4**

- Rosier - Demon of love: *Serena Alora Rosier Aken* - He often remains reclusive from the human eye. Most of his work is done from afar. Rosier does, however, answer prayers and listens quite well. On the Demonic plane he will stay bathed in a shadowed corner when introduced. He is very shy.
- Astarte - (Female) Demoness of love: *Serena Alora Astarte Aken*
- Ashtaroth - (Female) Priestess of friendship: *Tasa Alora foren Ashtaroth* -Twin to Astarot
- Astarot - Matters concerning the heart: *Serena Alora Astartot Aken* - Twin to Ashtaroth
- Amducious - The destroyer: *Denyen valocur avage secore Amducious* - Twin to Asmodeous. Direction: Southeast. Colors: Orange; Month: May; Season: Late Spring; Ritual: war, action, dispel old.
- Asmodeus - Demon of Lust: *Ayer avage Aloren Asmodeus aken* - Twin to Amducious. Appears as an attractive and clean cut and articulate man. His eyes seduce all women mortal and otherwise. He will answer calls by Ouija boards if asked. He is very friendly. Be forewarned, he often turns conversation into some aspect of sexuality as it pleases him.

## Family 5

- Eurynomous - Demon of Death: *Ayar Secore on ca Eurynomous* Direction: Northwest. Colors: Black and White; Month: October; Season: Late Autumn; Ritual: New beginnings, death, rebirth, celebration of death, Halloween. Eurynomous appears as a shadow or wraith. Or as a common man with white or translucent hair and pale or white eyes. His energy is calming and cool. He also holds the book of the dead. He often communicates vi baoith raimi Kairtey - or as invisible hands.
- Balberith - Prince of dying: *Avage Secoré on ca Baalberith* - He guides the souls of the dead to the Demonic plane where they are reborn from the whole of the fifth element. He leads them to safe passage. He appears as someone the deceased remembers who has also passed on. His true form is a mystery.
- Babeal - Keeper of Graves: *Alan Secore on ca Babeal* - He is a shadow amidst the graveyards tending souls and graves. Keeping them safe from desecration at their resting places.

## Family 6

- Verrine - Demon of Health: *Elan Typan Verrine* - Direction: Northwest; Colors: Blue, white; Month: November; Season: Late Autumn; Ritual: healing.
- Verrier - (Female) Demoness of herbal knowledge: *Elit Rayesta Verrier* - Direction: Northwest; Colors: Light Green; Month: November; Season: Late Autumn.; Ritual: healing, earth, knowledge or herbalism.
- Ronwe - Demon of Knowledge: *Kaymen Vefa Ronwe* - comes to those who seek him through

dreams in settings befitting the Demon of knowledge such as bookstores, libraries, and cafes where many intellectual types gather. His form varies often as he is an adept at changing his appearance. However, his demeanor remains consistent with that of the sage wise man. His soul is very old and his eyes reflect great understanding.

## Family 7

- Svengali - Demon of Vengeance: *Desa on Svengali ayer* - White hair, red eyes
- Tezrian - (Female) Priestess of battle: *Ezyr ramec ganen Tezrian*

**Family 8** - Some speculation has arisen suggesting that family 8 should actually be coupled with family 3. As it has been suggested these are the females of that family.

- Asafoetida - (Female) Demoness of feminine attributes: *Asana nanay on ca Asafoetida*
- Rashoon - (Female) Priestess of seduction: *Taran Rashoon nanay* - Twin to Taroon.
- Taroon - (Female) Priestess of Desire: *Taroon an ca nanay* - Twin to Rashoon.

## Family 9

Consists of lesser hierarchy: These are the only Enns I currently have of lesser hierarchs, or hierarchy that does not appear in the Dukante hierarchy.

Berith: *Hoath redar ganabal Berith*
Agares: *Rean ganen ayar da Agares*
Abigor: *Aylan Abigor tasa uan on ca*
Lillith:  *Renich viasa avage lillith lirach*

## Concerning the Enns

No one knows what language the Enns come from. Some have speculated they are in some form of Gaelic, but our research into that claim has proven that this is not the case. They were deemed Demonic Enns in late 16th Century by Demonolator Alexander Willit[4]. The Enns are unique in that they appear across several family grimoires (unless noted) that are from different geographic locations, and remain the same. This is also the case for the sigils for Demons of the Dukante Hierarchy. There are slight variations to the sigils but they remain very similar or largely the same. We'll show you this in the sigil section when we compare two sigils of Azlyn gotten through ascension by two different people in different geographic locations. There are also allegedly Enns for many of the Goetic Demons though I have not collected nor included them here.

## An Enn Dictionary

The following definitions were received from an ascension with Delepitorae. These are the only Enn related words we have been able to define so far. It's terribly short, I know.

Asta - Ashtaroth
Et – And
Fubin – (the) Flame
Ganic – Fire
Geana – Mystery
Jedan - Water
Hesta -  Curse
Hoet - Our

---

[4] From the Willit Family Grimoire circa 1648.

Lanire – Liar
Lirach – Earth
Naca – Circle (ring)
Par – Thee
Renich - Air
Roroth – (bring) to me
Tasa – Protect
Uberaca Biasa Icar – the Surrounding Sky
Vefa - This
Wehlc - Soil
Withar – Discover

## I don't have an Enn I need – what should I do?

This question comes up a lot, believe it or not. Your best bet is to design an invocation of your own. *"Lord Paimon, I seek you, please attend this rite."* This is a perfectly acceptable example of how to create your own invocation. Just remember to always be kind and respectful. Do not command the Demons! The reason for this will be explained in the section discussing proper invocation.

## Additional Hierarchy Correspondences

For reference, here are the nine divinities again. You will see this list repeated often throughout this book because they are important. Some people have chosen Goetic counterparts to the Nine that they feel fit the Dukante counterparts.

Satan
Lucifer
Flereous
Leviathan
Belial
Verrine

Amducious
Unsere
Eurynomous

## From the Purswell Grimoires- Elemental Breakdown

Satan-All
Belial/Eurynomous-Earth
Lucifer/Verrine-Air
Flereous/Amducious-Fire
Leviathan/Unsere  - Water

I, the author, have a theory about elemental and alchemical breakdown regarding the above elemental designations of The Nine.

- Satan: All
- Belial: Earth
- Lucifer: Air
- Flereous: Fire
- Leviathan: Water
- Unsere: Vapor (Fire transformed Water)
- Amducious: Heat (Air transformed Fire)
- Verrine: Cold (Water transformed Earth)
- Eurynomous: Dry (Earth transformed Air)

Please see the section on the Demonolatry Tree of Life and the Qlippoth for more on my own thoughts on this.

## From the Purswell Grimoires - Purpose Breakdown

| | |
|---|---|
| *Enlightenment*: | Lucifer/Belial/Satan |
| *Creative*: | Leviathan/Unsere/Verrine |
| *Destructive*: | Flereous/Amducious/Eurynomous |

**From Dukanté's Grimoire Book 7 Notes: Page 49 (Note: p/o is part of)**

Verrine = airy p/o water
Verrier = earthy p/o water
Leviathan = watery p/o water
Sonnellion = fiery p/o water
Ronwe = airy p/o earth
Belial = earthy p/o earth
Tezrian = fiery p/o earth
Unsere = watery p/o earth
Lucifuge = earthy p/o air
Lucifer = airy p/o air
Ammon = fiery p/o air
Delepitorae = watery p/o air
Belphegore = earthy p/o fire
???? = airy p/o fire
Flereous = fiery p/o fire
Amducuious = watery p/o fire

*Page 73*

**Water**= Sonnellion, Verrine, Verrier, Leviathan, Delepitorae
**Earth** = Baalberith, Unsere, Eurynomous, Belphagore, Babael, Ronwe
**Air** = Lucifer, Lucifuge Rofocale
**Fire** = Asmodeous, Tezrian

[Note: This section of the text was incomplete, because Dukanté hadn't finished his classifications. Also note there are inconsistencies with where Tezrian belongs. Fire or Earth]

*Concerning the Commanders: Pages 163-164*

Satanchia is the tallest. He bears the mark of Satan, his father, on the small of his left back. He carries himself proudly, with dark hair and eyes, a mustache and hair that falls to his shoulders.

Lucifuge Rofocale is much shorter. His eyes glow green and he has sharp nails. He, more so than the others, looks fiendish.

Agaliarept is the most sedate of the three brothers. His hair and eyes are brown. He is slender and tall and quite unassuming.

*Concerning the Elementals: Pages 165-173*

Elemental Demons are very distinguishable, not because of their overall appearance, but because of their eyes. They are entrancing, cat-like. They glow and are very large. Elementals also give off bright rays of energy with colors corresponding to their element. They stand very tall and most often visit humans in their dreams.

*Females in the Dukanté Hierarchy Page 173*

The Females of the 5th and 8th families appear as the viewer wishes them to appear. To the male they often appear as a beautiful woman, to the female a half-cat/half woman, or just as women.

## Dukante Excerpts from Book 18 – Observations

Page 12: Demons that can give sigils of personal power (vi baoith Raimi Kairtey) include only the nine Demonic divinities.

Page 17: Sleeping with the sigil of a specific Demon beneath your mattress or pillow will increase your chances of meeting a Demon during a dream state.

Page 47: Start your invitational enns kneeling on your left knee. Trace the symbol or sigil, kiss the blade, raise the blade above your head, push it upward, then down in one even stroke without jabbing or thrusting. This is the most pleasing form of inviting a Demon into a circle. All priesthood should take measure to do this.

Page 94: It is always more powerful to construct circles from your own elemental point.

Pages 163-164 - Of Satanchia/Agaliarept and other Militia Demons.

3 Military Powers of the Demonic Plane:

    Gog - they are legion
    Mingog - offensive
    Dilgog - defensive

3 Commanders of these powers:
  Satanchia
  Lucifuge
  Agaliarept

# Sigils

We'll start with the Dukante Hierarchy.

Like I mentioned in the previous chapter, the sigils were also gotten from ascended states. We have a modern example of this and it's really quite interesting. Two Demonolators in different States believed they had each gotten sigil of Azlyn via ascension. Azlyn is a recent addition to the Dukante hierarchy and we had a description of her and an Enn, but we had no sigil. Each Demonolatress sent her sigil to me. These women got their sigils at different times and neither knew the other had one. This is what I received.

While they aren't exactly alike, notice the similar shape (a diagonal V), the two right-hand cross lines in the lower right of each sigil, and the fact that both have loops (albeit in different spots). I've been told there are a few variations like this for each sigil, but the basic shape is always the same and the sigils will share two or more similar characteristics like loops or cross lines. The rest of the sigils on the following pages were gotten via ascension like this. I am not sure if it was Dukante who got them or if he copied them from another grimoire. I have heard no complaints. What I do know is that I got them from Dukante's grimoires and have printed them here with the permission of his daughter. We'll start with all the sigils you may have seen if you've seen any of the other books they're printed in. Please forgive the formatting after these because the remaining sigil graphics were done separately.

Sigils are signatures - representations - pictographs - that represent an individual or entity. They are symbols of our own design by which to focus on. We utilize them during ritual and in image to honor the Demons and Ourselves.

### Burn that Sigil - The Hell You Say?

I think the most common question I hear when people begin practicing Demonolatry is, *"I have to burn the sigil??!!!"* followed by a gasp. As students, we were all once concerned about burning sigils. It made us sick to our stomachs. Nervous, and maybe even a little wary for several days following the unspeakable act. We learned this by our other occult studies where reading scores of books that told us burning a sigil was sacrilege, and it was how we controlled Demons. That burning the sigil made the Demon angry with us. Or that it gave the Demon its power back because we no longer held its sigil.

In Demonolatry, Sigils are burned. They are given to the flames during ritual, or buried in the ground as a symbolic offering of our devotion. By doing this, we are not destroying anything sacred. We are simply rendering the sigil or request during a rite to share our devotion to the entity for which it was created. By committing the sigil to fire you are symbolically changing its form and allowing your message to rise, like the phoenix, to a state of energy so that the Demons can absorb the positive energy put forth in its creation.

Satanchia

Lucifer

Mesphito

Agaliarept

Beelzebuth

Delepitorae

Flereous

Belphegore

Leviathan

Ammon

Astarte

Baalberith

Mammon

Asmodeus

Ronwe

Rosier

Eurynomous

Teznan

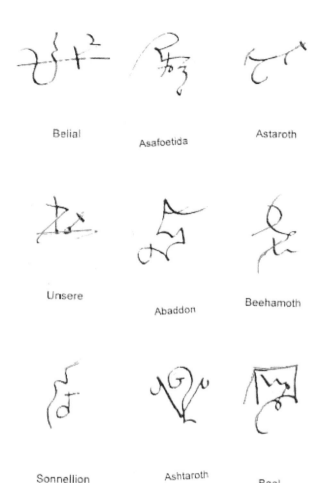

Belial

Asafoetida

Astaroth

Unsere

Abaddon

Beehamoth

Sonnellion

Ashtaroth

Baal

Amducious

Lucifuge

Satan

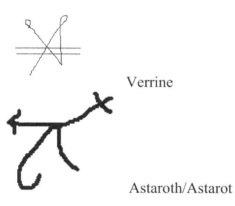

This invocation sigil can also be used to represent Satan or any of the Nine Divinities. See the section on Invocation to learn more about the invocation sigil.

Verrine

Astaroth/Astarot

Verrier

Abigor

Balandax  –  not actually listed in the hierarchy, but among the sigils.

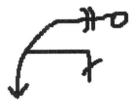

Boragus  –  not actually listed in the hierarchy, but among the sigils.

Lilith

Luithian

Rashoon

Svengali

S. Connolly

Taroon

## Circled Sigils vs. Un-circled Sigils

A sigil is often circled in Demonolatry to denote Satan encompassing that particular part of the whole. By circling the sigil you are focusing on the Demon as part of something larger. By leaving the sigil un-circled it suggests focusing on the Demon itself without looking at it as part of the whole. Think of it as zooming in or out. If you want to see the larger picture – circle it. If you want to hone in on the Demon itself, don't.

In Goetic and Ceremonial Magick, encircling the sigil is often symbolic of having power over a Demon. Demonolators **do not** do this. We do not see ourselves as above the Demons. It is considered disrespectful, and it *can* get you into trouble with Demons. Never use Demonolatry based practices or magick and then attempt to bind or control a Demon. The author of this book is not responsible for your actions and does not guarantee your safety if you stray from the guidelines for respectful Demon worship as contained within this book.

# Goetic Hierarchy Sigils

### Bael

### Agares

### Vassago

### Gamigin

## Marbas

## Valefor

## Amon

## Barbatos

## Paimon

## Buer

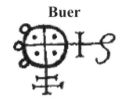

## Gusion

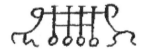

## Sitri/Sytry

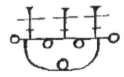

## Beleth

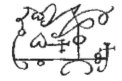

## Leraje

## Elgios

## Zepar

## Botis

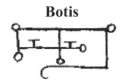

## Bathin

## Sallos

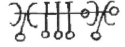

## Purson

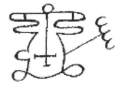

## Marax

## Ipos

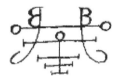

## Aim

## Naberius

## Glasya-Labolas

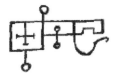

## Bune

## Ronove

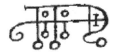

## Berith

## Astaroth

## Forneus

## Foras

## Asmoday

# Gaap

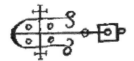

# Furfur

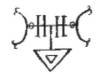

# Marchosias

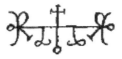

# Stolas

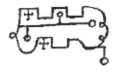

## Phenex

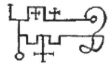

## Halphas

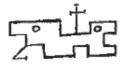

## Malphas

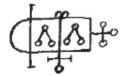

## Raum

## Focalor

## Vepar

## Sabnock

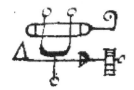

## Shax

## Vine

## Bifrons

## Uvall

## Haagenti

## Crocell

## Furcus

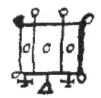

## Balam

## Alloces

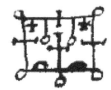

## Caim

## Murmur

## Orobas

## Gremory

## Ose

## Amy

## Orias

## Vapula

## Zagan

## Volac

## Andras

## Haures

## Andrealphus

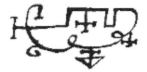

## Cimejes

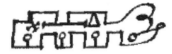

## Amducious.

## Belial

## Decarabia

## Seere

## Dantalion

## Andromalius

# The Basics of Hermetics

## The Foundations of Demonolatry

The Religions and theosophy of Ancient Egypt is the source and foundation of Demonolatry. The Egyptian Gnostic/Hermetic tradition birthed two schools. The first was the Philosophical and Alchemical Schools (from a scientific standpoint) and second were the Spiritual Schools that also included the philosophical and alchemical (from a more spiritual standpoint). Demonolatry, many believe, is a direct descendant from the Spiritual Schools of the Ancient teachings of Egypt, which may or may not have come from an even earlier culture.

Many Greeks went to Egypt and learned from the Illuminati of the Egyptian Temples. From this, the Egyptian theosophy and alchemical studies of Hermetics came to be known in the classical world from the writings of many Greek philosophers. Alchemy birthed physics, biology, and psychology during the enlightenment.

It was from the Philosophical Schools of Ancient Egypt that birthed medieval Freemasonry, of which the Knights Templar are a subset. From the Spiritual Schools (aside from Demonolatry) also came Rosicrucianism. There is a reason the Masons and Rosicrucians are often linked. It is because they come from sister schools in different subsets of the same tradition. The higher-ranking degree members of both the Masons and the Rosicrucians make up the fabled Illuminati. Contrary to popular belief that the Illuminati is a secret society of its own (which at one time was allegedly true), there is some evidence that it could actually be a melding of the Masons' and Rosicrucians' higher orders. Illuminati is a title given those persons who, in either tradition, have become enlightened to Gnosis; Universal Consciousness.

In the tradition of separate schools, the Masons ended up birthing mundane (of earth) magickal traditions (with influences from an indirectly Egypt influenced Arabic Magick) like the OTO and other less spiritual forms of ceremonial magick where the goal is to envoke from within the Self for the purpose of psychological development of internal wisdom, whereas from Rosicrucianism we get Enochian Magick (John Dee was allegedly a Rosicrucian) and subsequently the Golden Dawn which are forms of magick more spiritually linking the Self to Universal Consciousness and the elements of creation. Also, Modern Druidism, Alexandrian Witchcraft and thus Modern Day Wicca all have direct links to Rosicrucianism with regards to the mystical, more new age type studies. The founder of Alexandrian Witchcraft was a Rosicrucian. In these three modern examples – the Hermetic/Alchemical, Scientific, and in some cases the Theosophical has all been wiped away or is not explored as thoroughly as the tradition that influenced it. Other Modern Occult Movements that were influenced either directly or indirectly by the Rosicrucians and Masons and consequently Ancient Egypt, include Modern Khemetic groups, Thelema, Temple of Set, Gnostic Luciferianism et al. And all are valid paths.

Because knowledge and spirituality do not exist in a vacuum, the teachings of both schools (Philosophical/Scientific and Spiritual) have expanded their teachings in new traditions, deleted those things that no longer apply, and have come a long way from their ancestor schools, but the basic underlying theosophical, hermetic, and alchemical teachings are still intact and grow as we learn more about science and the nature of the universe we live in. Consequently, as previously mentioned, the magickal and spiritual teachings have grown to include modern applications.

For Example: Whereas 6000 years ago you might have blessed and protected your livestock, nowadays you might bless and protect your car. This is what we mean by saying these traditions, by whatever name their movement founder gives them, modernize for the society in which they exist.

The ties that bind all of these traditions together is deeply rooted in Gnostic teaching and leads each of them straight back to Ancient Egypt even if they have strayed off the basic path of the ancient schools. Undoubtedly the popular religions of our modern world have also been influenced by these ancient teachings. It is highly apparent in their rituals, texts, and practices to those who have been properly trained to see the ancient traditions and ideology within. That is not to say *all* things in modern religion can be found in the ancient schools. Many modern paths have taken what they found useful and left the rest behind.

While Demonolatry may have not been known as Demonolatry as it is today, the fact still remains that the basic underlying teachings of the ancient schools are still there. We have not left behind as much as some of the others. Demonolator is simply a modern label used to describe one who communes, worships, and seeks wisdom from divine intelligences (Daimons, Daemons, and Demons). Divine intelligence can also come from the Self via an inherent wisdom we each possess, which is one of the most basic teachings of the Ancient Egyptians – that we are as Gods and also Divine by the very substance of our beings.

## What is Hermeticism?

Hermeticism is a theosophy explaining the science of the universe, the nature of the Gods, and man's place within the universe. The Scientifica Hermetica, written by Hermes Trismegistus as his interpretation of the teachings of Ancient Egypt's Papyri of Ani. Hermeticism can be linked as the forefather to all modern religions, and is the basis for many modern day schools of occult thought including Demonolatry and the various forms of Ceremonial Magick including Enochian and Qabbalah (from the Jewish mysticism).

## From Ancient Egypt to Greek Philosophy

The Hermetic theosophy was taken to Greece by way of the numerous Greek philosophers who traveled to ancient Egypt in order to learn from the priests in the temples. The priests were thought to have sacred knowledge passed on from an even older culture.

**Practical Modern Hermetic Science**

From Hermetic Science, alchemy, came modern Chemistry and Physics. You can also see, if you read the texts carefully, the ancient understanding of astronomy and the creation of the universe. Strangely this information has been in front of us for centuries, but it took modern science's rediscovery of it for us to realize it was something our ancestors already knew. So while you read the following books, keep in mind the metaphors used and how they might be applied to common scientific knowledge we each now possess. For example – how our earth revolves around our sun.

**Reading Assignments:** Read the following books when you get a chance. They will give you a strong foundation of the basis for Demonolatry. I believe that many of you reading this will likely find yourself enlightened by this material.

- **Hermetica:The Greek Corpus Hermeticum -** by Hermes Trismegistus
- **The Hermetica – Lost Wisdom of the Pharaohs** by Freke & Gandy
- **Initiation Into Hermetics** – by Franz Bardon
- **The Egyptian Book of the Dead** – the Budge translation is fine, but if you can find a different translation, consider that. While Budge is considered the expert in Egyptology, it has recently come to light that some of his translations were wrong and they are quite Christian, as Atem (the source of all and synonymous with Satan) is often called God, in the generic sense at best.

**The Scientific Design of Deity**

The Hermetica explains the scientific design and nature of Deities as the sentient, though sometimes chaotic and unpredictable forces of nature and natural elements occurring in our world and beyond. This is further corresponded to alchemical properties metaphoric to the nature of the spiritual, thus connecting it to the mundane. All the while, Deity is bound much by the same physical laws of nature our modern science has defined with regards to basic physics. There are also laws we don't understand. Consider String Theory in how various dimensions vibrate at different frequencies, binding matter together to make up our universe. I strongly recommend Stephen Hawking's *A Brief History of Time*. The Enochian Theorums, written by John Dee, also influenced by Hermetic thinking, are simply his summaries of theorums written by Hermes Trismegistus in the Hermetica, taken from the natural laws observed by the ancient Egyptians.

**Matter cannot be created or destroyed, it can only change form**.

The form of Deity is infinite. Many people look at Demons and believe a Demon can only be at one place at one time. Therefore they think a Demon cannot come to them and be expected to be with another at the same time. As humans, we oftentimes think too small. We look at anything that physically exists in our world and know it has shape and size and can only be in one place at one time. Even in the case of physical manifestation. So we carry that over to the supernatural world and expect that all things we cannot necessarily see must also be contained in a single physical shape or form. It's just the nature of our thinking based on our knowledge and experience of our physical form. We like to give our gods (Daemon or other) physical shape and form in our own image so that we may better identify with that which we do not understand. It gives us a point of reference with which to conceptualize the nature of deity. But there's an innate problem with that line of limited and biased human thinking.

My experience tells me, and therefore I believe, the Demons themselves are an interwoven part of our natural universe. Not only could they realistically be multi-dimensional, but they could very well transcend the boundaries of time and space and all laws of physics as we know them. Their exact nature is beyond human comprehension. Their popularity notwithstanding, some Demons are so ever present that they can exist in all things at once. In Demonolatry we believe They are just as much a part of us as we are Them. Therefore it is perfectly plausible that a Demon can be in multiple places at once and can manifest simultaneously.

# History

## Yezidiz - Demon Worship in Russia and Syria Dating to the 13th Century

If you were to read the Black Book (dating to the 13th century) of the Yezidiz, the seasoned occult scholar would immediately be able to clearly define the roles of Demons, although differently named, in the Yezidiz tradition. The Yezidiz is a small sect comprised of approximately 200,000 followers. Like many Demonolatry Sect traditions, the Yezidiz pass their faith to each subsequent generation creating a strong generational priesthood as a result. The Sect was studied extensively in the late 19th and early 20th century by theologists from across the globe who found interesting similarities to Christianity within the religious structure of the Sect. Some speculate the sect is much older than Christianity and conformed some of its original traditions to the mold of the Christian ways in order that they might survive the Christian onset. Aside from Christian tradition there are also traces of Moslem and Persian influence. There are nine positive influence "arch-angels" or "Demonic entities" worshipped by the Yezidiz. They are:

> Shams El Din
> Fakr El Ein
> Nasr El Din
> Sij El Din
> Sheikh Ism
> Sheikh Bakra
> Kadir Rahman

While there is little documentation of true Demonolatry sects in history, the Yezidiz, although obscure, remain the best-documented and researched Demonolatry sect of all time outside the Demonolatry community.

## The Knights Templar

Between the years of 1119 and 1188 a small group of knights founded the Knights Templar also known as The Order in dedication to protect pilgrims traveling to the holy land. Originally a Christian Order, the Templars held their religious rites in much secrecy. Because of this secrecy much speculation occurred regarding their nature as a religious order. Rumors that had been brewing for generations suggested the Templars worshiped Baphomet and partook in satanic rites during these secret meetings. Others believe the rumors were a product of King Philip IV of France who desperately sought to remove the power of the Templars not only for his own sake (as he owed them a substantial sum of money), but for his alleged dislike of one of the Order's Grand Masters. Still other sources suggest that while the Order was originally Christian it was overtook by the de Lemann Sect in 1249 and was a true

Demonolatry Sect.[5] In the latter instance it is stated the reason the Templars fell was due to a loosening of the secrecy factor among members and less rigid entry requirements, which allowed almost any man to join the order providing he was willing.

While the individual members of the Order were quite poor, the Order gained excessive wealth, which they used in commerce. By the 14th Century the Order was a financial and religious power whose only contender was the Pope himself. In 1307 King Philip IV convinced Pope Clement to have all the Templars arrested. The Templars were stripped of all their properties and titles and were tried for sorcery and heresy and burnt at the stake. The Order was dissolved on an official level by Philip in 1312.

Only the latter we can be sure of, for the persecution of the Templars is well documented. However, whether or not the Templars were a genuine Demonolatry Sect remains speculation and theory. Their rites were not documented in public file. Much of the testimony of the occurrences at these secret meetings was given under extreme torture and interrogation and is therefore deemed invalid due to circumstance.

## Demonic Possession

Here we shall take a look at Demon possession hysteria. The primary (and perhaps best known) incidents that should be mentioned here are the Louviers Possessions, the Aix Possessions, and the Loudon Possessions.

---

[5] From the Delaney Family Grimoire circa 1519.

**LOUVIERS**: The possessions at Louviers took place at the Louviers Convent in 1647. Much like the Aix and Loudun Possession cases, Father Mathurin Picard (nunnery director) and Father Thomas Boulle (vicar at Louviers) were convicted on the evidence of the possessed nuns. Sister Madeleine Bavent, who was eighteen years old at the time, was the initial possession victim whose testimony threw the church into a panic. Supposedly, Picard and Boulle had taken the nuns to secret sabbats where they cavorted with Demons; Namely the Demon Dagon by Bavent's testimony. Similar testimony of the other nuns followed. Upon further investigation it was discovered that the nuns were suffering from the classic symptoms of possession.

**Demonic Possession - The Classic Symptoms**

- Contortions
- Unnatural body movements.
- Speaking in tongues (glossolalia)
- Insults
- Blasphemies
- Appearance of wounds that vanish as quickly as they appear.

As at Loudun, the exorcism rites at Louviers were made public. Accounts of the incident suggest the exorcism was anything but a holy ritual. The inquisitors allegedly created mass hysteria questioning and harassing everyone. Father Boulle was tortured during the exorcism.

Parliament at Rouen's Sentence, Sister Bavent was imprisoned for life, Father Boulle was burnt alive, and the corpse of Father Picard (who was fortunate enough to have died earlier) was exhumed and burned.

**LOUDUN:** This has been deemed the most famous case of possession hysteria in history. In 1634, it was said Father Urbain Grandier inflicted possession onto the Ursuline nuns of Loudun. This is the case that questioned the actual existence of Demonic possession, whether or not the nuns had indeed been suffering, and whether or not Father Grandier had died for reasons other than the possessions (namely political reasons). Accusations against Father Grandier began with Mother Superior Jeanne des Agnes who reported having illicit and Demonic dreams featuring Grandier. No amount of penance kept Jeanne's dreams at bay, and soon - the other nuns had followed suit - succumbing to the hysteria of the Mother Superior's dreams and having their own. At this point, it is reported that Father Mignon, an enemy of Grandier, and his assistant took the alleged possessions as an opportunity to turn against Grandier. They began exorcising the nuns. Two of the Demons namely responsible for these possessions were Asmodeus and Zabulon although there were others.

Grandier ordered the nuns isolated and wrote to the Archbishop of Bordeaux, who in turn, immediately sent a doctor to examine the nuns. The doctor found the women physically sound and free from possession. Regardless, Grandier let stay his order that the nuns be confined to their cells. This quieted the hysteria for a few months, but then it started again.

This time, Grandier's enemies were working to have him arrested and convicted of witchcraft. Former lovers of Grandier came forth with stories of sacrilege, adultery, and incest. Meanwhile, Jeanne continued feeding the hysteria - adding names to the roster of Demons possessing the nuns. She even went as far as to go through a psychosomatic pregnancy.

**The Demons on the Loudun possession roster:**

Asmodeus, Zabulon, Isacaaron, Astaroth, Gresil, Amand, Leviatom, Behemot, Beherie, Easas, Celsus, Acaos, Cedon, Alex, Naphthalim, Cham, Ureil, and Achas.

Finally, Grandier was charged, tortured, convicted, and sentenced to be burned alive. The nuns were supposedly exorcised by Father Surin, a renowned exorcist who later succumbed to the very Demons he banished, having gone insane. Invariably, the possessions at the Loudun convent continued (supposedly as a tourist attraction since the exorcisms drew so much attention) even after Grandier's death. The possessions finally stopped in 1637 when the fraud was uncovered.

**AIX-EN-PROVENCE:** The incident at Aix (burning Father Gaufridi alive) acted as the precedent setting case for the Loudun Possessions' conviction and sentence of Father Grandier twenty years later. This is also the first case where the testimony of a possessed person was taken into account during the conviction of Father Gaufridi. Prior to the seventeenth century, a possessed person's testimony was not used since Demons were known to be liars.

As in the Loudun possessions, sexual themes played a large role in the possession testimony. Father Gaufridi was convicted by his own confessions (under torture) as well as the testimonies of the possessed nuns, Sister Madeleine Demandolx de la Palud and Sister Louise Capel. Both Father Gaufridi and Sister Madeleine recited their denouncement of god and the saints before the church.

The Verdict and Aftermath: Father Gaufridi was burnt alive. Both nuns were banished from the convent. In 1613, two years later, the possession hysteria spread to nearby Lille. In Lille it was reported that three nuns were possessed. They accused Sister Marie de Sains of bewitching them.

## Brief Analysis of Demonic Possession Cases:

The above possession cases are interesting in their similarities. Is it possible that nunneries were suspect to Demon possession due to the sexual frustration of the chaste women of God? This is a real probability knowing the psychology of human instinct.

Could the Priests have been sexual deviants? Maybe, however it seems unlikely. If that were the case, wouldn't the nuns in each case merely have turned the offending priest into the church hierarchy for breaking his vows and for sexually exploiting the women? Many people are inclined to believe so. Some people conclude that women were not as oppressed as we are led to believe by modern history texts.

Is there such a thing as Demon possession? Who knows. There is so much about the world we do not understand. What is possible is only within the realm of human perception. Whatever that perception is relies exclusively on each individual. However, most Demonolators are doubtful that Demons would bother possessing humans unless there is some driving need that exceeds recommendation for physical manifestation.

### Richard Dukanté

Perhaps one of the foremost Demonolators renowned today is the late Richard Dukanté. Dukanté was born in 1931 in Chicago, Illinois to Andrew and Teresa Dukanté. He was raised a traditional Demonolator and attended private schools. Having been raised among the social scene of the occult community he had the pleasure of meeting numerous occult personalities from his early teen years onward. Among them, Aleister Crowley in 1945 just two years before Crowley's demise.

In 1952, when he was merely 21, Dukanté's mother died in an automobile accident and not a year later, with a bad heart, his father followed. His sister, Elizabeth (b1933), had since renounced her family for their religious practices and had married into a Christian family. It was at this time Dukanté began his immersion into Demonolatry. After obtaining a masters degree in Theology with extensive studies in Latin and History from Princeton, he supported himself as a private tutor and lived off the trust fund and inheritance his parents left him.

In 1960, Dukanté married Laura Emmery and in 1965 he fathered his first and only child, Selinda Tezrian Dukanté. Dukanté's zealousness for Demonolatry and his obscure practices led his wife to divorce him in 1968 at which time he was granted custody of his daughter. In 1967 Dukanté, along with several members of the Demonolatry priesthood [Delaney, Purswell, Linton, and Willit], started the early Guild of Demonolatry. In 1968 the Shadow Guild of Demonolatry (SGD) was officially established with a membership exceeding 50 people. It was 1963 when the Dukanté Hierarchy was first established complete with female Demons other than commonalties such as Lilith. Dukanté claimed he had found a way, through ritual, that allowed him to travel to Demonic planes of existence where he recorded the physical description of the Demons as he was introduced to them. He claimed Satan, himself, had escorted these brief, but numerous tours.

For this he received much ridicule from the occult community. Two of his closest confidants, also Demonolators, who stood by him during this trying time, were Lance Delaney and Grant Purswell. By 1980, Dukanté had been labeled a lunatic by numerous occultists and Demonolators alike. He died in 1985 at the age of 54, from a heart attack. During his life, Dukanté put together over 25 unpublished books detailing his workings and experiments with Demons. These books have come to be known, within the Demonolatry community, as the Dukanté Grimoires.

# Historic Timeline
## Significant Events in Demonolatry History

**3000BC** - The Hermetica - a collection of writings attributed to Thoth, is the basis for Modern day Demonolatry philosophy. These writings are dated to a least 3000 BC. Egyptian, Greek, and Roman religions along with practices of the Caananites, Amorites and other various sects are the forefathers of Demonolatry. Note the similarities (i.e. people chose patrons/matrons and worked with pantheons being among the most obvious).

**2500BC** - The Amorites worshiped BaalBerith at the same time the Canaanites and Semites worshiped Baal. The earliest known versions of rites done to these particular deities do in fact date historically to around 1400 BC according to texts found at Rad Shamara in 1929.

**AD onward** - The Onslaught of Christianity - the Demonic Gods of the old religions become "devils". Please note that by saying Demonic - I mean these gods are divine intelligences replete with wisdom. Divine coming from the Latin Divus. Demonolatry goes underground.

**100-400 AD**- Testament of Solomon appears with the instructions to command the Djinn. Notice how Solomon was never accused of witchcraft, but will always be remembered as the wise king even though he allegedly worked with Demons closely for some years. From this appears the Goetic hierarchy for which all modern grimoires (Grand Grimoire, Black Pullet et al) are derived from. Same stuff, different books.

**1119AD - 1188AD** - Knights Templar were said to worship Baphomet. Historically they were a Christian order and allegedly a subset of the Masons, but many people still suggest that the order was a bonified Demonolatry sect. The Delaney Family Grimoire circa 1519 discusses the Templars as a valid Demonolatry sect by saying: "Whilst the Templars are not of our family, we shall treat them as such as we pay our respects to Baphomet in their sacred temples." [page 90, book 2]

**1200 AD** - The Yezidiz (Yezidis) tradition [Syria and Russia] is first documented in family grimoires. Demons were worshipped as rulers of the earth. The Yezidis believed that if they worshipped Demons while they were alive their crops would be fine and they would be spared plagues. But they also believed that when they died they would go to heaven. Their idea - worship the rulers of the earth (Demons) while on earth - worship God in the afterlife.

**1312 AD** - The Nine Demonic Divinities (with obvious Christian influence to some degree) appears in the Black Book (Grimoire) of Thoman Buchan.

**1589 -1863AD** - A Demon becomes synonymous with devil when numerous members of the Christian Clergy create hierarchies of Demons using the names of the old

Gods. Demonolators pretend to be Christian just so they won't be murdered.

**1585AD** - or thereabouts - Demonolator Alexander Willit deems the strange invocations used by Demonolators - Demonic Enns. No one knows for sure what language the Enns are in. However, one thing is for sure - the Enns scattered throughout the world in various unrelated family grimoires from different time periods all remain the SAME. There is a consistency there that tells us something deeper is at work here.

**1963AD** - Richard Dukante creates the first Demonic hierarchy put together by a Demonolator. Starts the SGD, a worldwide network of Demonolatry Sects.

**1985AD**- Dukante dies.

**1997AD**- Tezrian's Vault is born as a public voice for the Demonolatry community (even as small as it may be).

**1998AD** - Demonolatry.com is born and Demonolatry has a public voice on a larger scale.

**1999AD** - The first book on Demonolatry written by a Demonolator is published. Modern Demonolatry, Darkerwood Publishing 1999.

**2000AD** - The first "public" sect is born in the First Temple of Demonolatry.

**2001AD** - Demonolatry goes back underground. Goes off of the Internet because of misconceptions. The First Temple of Demonolatry is disbanded.

# The Old Grimoires

- Key of Solomon - This book is referred to in many historical documents from the 1st century onward. Thus, historians believe this manuscript was in existence in the 1st century. There is a Greek version of this text dating 1100-1200 in the British Museum. Other known publication dates include around 1345, 1555, and in the 17 Century it was quite popular. You can get copies of this book translated by Crowley and Mathers from Samuel Weiser publishing. These books are readily available at amazon.com or any major bookseller in the occult section.

- Grimorium Verum - a lot of people believe this one was actually written in the 18th century even though it's alleged date (as you well know) is 1517. IGOS and Trident publishing each have a version.

- Honorius - showed up in Rome in the early to mid 1600's. It was also popular in the 17th century. Trident has a version of this.

- Abremalin - many people think this book was written in the 18th century like Grimoirium Verum. It is rumored to have been written around 1450. Readily available from any large bookseller. I believe Weiser publishes this one.

- Grand Grimoire & Red Dragon are almost identical. Grand Grimoire is known to have been written in the 17th century. While the Red Dragon is an 19th (1822) century work claiming to have roots back in 1522. Books can be obtained through IGOS, Trident, and sometimes-major booksellers. Check with Amazon.com

All of these grimoires have pretty much the same information in them. If you want a composite - try AE Waite's Book of Black Magic (also Book of Ceremonial Magic) because it has a little of everything in it.

## Remy's Demonolatry

On first glance, one would look at Remy's Demonolatry and say, "Hey, this is just another witch hunting guide!" While this may be true, there are some interesting tidbits in this book making it a worthwhile study for someone who seriously wants to delve into a research project. Some Demonolators suggest Remy either got hold of a true grimoire and perverted it with old Christian claims of witchcraft OR he knew something of pre-Christian polytheistic and pantheistic ritual practice.

My personal opinion is that Remy simply referred to so many different sources that it was by pure coincidence that certain "not as well known facts about certain Demonolatry rites" got into the book. The book is filled with fascinating tidbits of Roman and Greek mythology, ritual practice and whatnot. That in and of itself qualifies it as a worthwhile peruse. You can take the dates and references and further research the subject matter to find more.

- Page 2 Chapter 2 - References to powders et al. While Demonolatry does use herbalism in some of its rites, I doubt this means anything. I've gone over it about six or seven times.

- Page 8 Chapter 5 - References to the Baphometic Fire Baptism rites that can be found in the Purswell grimoires and the Dukante grimoires. Remy doesn't come right out and say it was Baphometic. But he does refer to the "devil's mark" as a baptism mark (which is curious since most of the witch hunters referred to them as witches marks or devils marks). Obvious to me, Remy was referring to natural markings rather than obvious ones. Demonolatry baptismal markings are generally very obvious. Outside the interesting referral - this just goes into the poor method of how they used to test witches marks.

- Page 37 - For some reason I have this page marked. I think it was because the mention of drawing blood in honor of the Goddess Bellonarii. The drawing of blood from the arm instead of the palm is consistent with several of the rites in Grant's older grimoires. I think I was going to do some research on rites to Bellonarii.

- Page 40 Chapter 11- Making yearly offerings to their Demons. Some sects still practice this. This is the section about the black hens, goats, cattle and so forth. But, traditionally Black was used to absorb negative energy. The sacrifice was an offering to the Sect's Patron Demon, yet the sect consumed the sacrifice after the rite. During this particular rite (in the Purswell grimoires) all Sect members plucked hair from their head and placed them on the altar along with coins, herbal mixtures, and other offerings. All of the offerings were then tied up in a white cloth and buried at the foot of the altar.

- Page 41, Chapter 11 - Discusses Roman beliefs and how they qualify as "Demonolatry".

- Page 70-71 Chapter 23 - Discusses how Demons appear differently to everyone, which is true.

- Page 103, Book 2, Chapter 4 - Some historical mythology about Asmodeous.

- Page 113, Book 2, Chapter 113 - More fun mythology, this time about werewolves.

- Page 125 has some interesting cursing history on it. Obviously you can see the similarities to modern magick (regardless of tradition).

- Page 151, Book 2, Chapter 3 - Interesting Roman and Greek references discussing ritual practices. This book is laden with them.

- Page 153, Book 2, Chapter 3 - To obtain health it is said the Demon worshipper has angered the Demon "... therefore he [Demon] must be appeased by a votive pilgrimage to his shrine and by gifts and **nine days** sacrifices." This was a common practice.

- Page 176, Book 2, Chapter 11 - Discusses divination with the aid of Demons and again, how Demons show themselves to humans.

There were more pages than this marked, but these are the most interesting. You really have to dig into Remy and his footnotes to find tiny, little facts that coincide with some of the older Demonolatry grimoires. A lot of it can be applied it to any poly or pantheistic religion.

# The Hermetica - The Lost Wisdom of the Pharaohs

## From: "Man is a Marvel"

*For Reference - please note this is how I am interpreting this. Satan = Atum = the Cosmos = The Whole*

*Atum is first*
*the Cosmos is second*
*and man is third.*
*Atum is one.*
*The cosmos is one.*
*and so is man.*
*for like the Cosmos*
*he is a whole made up*
*of different diverse parts.*

This above segment explains how everything is part of the whole and how each part is just as important as the next.

*To speak without fear*
*human beings are above the gods of heaven*
*or at least their equal*

*By Atums will*
*humankind is compacted*
*of both divinity and mortality*
*He is more than merely mortal*
*and greater than the purely immortal.*

*Man is a marvel*
*due honor and reverence*

S. Connolly

*he takes on the attributes of gods*
*as if he were one of their number*
*He is familiar with the gods*
*because he knows he springs*
*from the same source*

These above segments explain sect law and how man is just as worthy of reverence as his gods. It also indicative of self-worship, the main qualifier of a LHP religion. This would suggest that the Egyptians were the first real LHP practitioners.

I highly recommend **The Hermetica: Lost Wisdom of the Pharaohs** by *Freke and Gandy*. It's short, comprehensive, and gives a basic alchemical introduction to Hermetic theosophy. For those of you who are studying for your initiation, please read it and make notes of the correlations you find as well as your thoughts and observations. For more advanced students, ponder how the text can be applied to modern science and the alchemical process of spiritual growth.

# The Practice of Demonolatry

Now that we've spent time discussing what Demonolatry is, Demons, their nature, sigils, Enns, the history behind Demonolatry, and that history illustrated in some obscure places, let's move on to what you have been waiting for – the actual practice of Demonolatry. If you are a beginner and have immediately jumped to this section, please go back. A lot of the information after this point will be better understood if you have a basic understanding of the aforementioned chapters. I realize it's a lot of information and many people are tempted to jump right in.

But I promise that if you understand the history, the nature of Demons, what Demonolatry is, sigils, and Enns you will get far more from your Demonolatry practice.

## The Coven/Sect

Demonolatry has been underground for centuries. In Europe, sects met in forest groves and caves in secret, teaching the ways of Demonolatry verbally. Allegedly few, if any, Demonolators were persecuted during the inquisition. By then, the secrecy factor with its rigid ways had been well built into the foundation of the religion. Some grimoires tell of Demonolators feigning being Christian for the sake of not arousing suspicions.

For this reason, written history of Demonolatry remains hidden in family grimoires long held clandestine over the centuries. Several written accounts elude to the fact that some people may have been aware of the existence of Demonolatry without having any real, concrete proof to go on. Perhaps the most famous incident was the torturous means by which the secret rituals of the Knight's Templar were unveiled during the height of the middle ages. While embellished to include Christian perversion, the described rites of the Templars, who allegedly worshipped Baphomet, are very close to actual Demonolatry rites of that time period. Sheep and hens were common sacrifices as were oxen and cattle. However, in almost all incidents of sacrifice a feast followed wherein the sacrifice was consumed by the Coven/Sect as the blood was the only part that could be used during ritual to any advantage. The blood of the sacrifice was made into magical inks and oleums and used as an offering to the Demonic entities.

Few Coven/Sects, if any, still use sacrifice as a common ritual practice. It should be noted here that humans are not and have never been sacrificed by Demonolatry sects. The easiest to obtain and perhaps the most common choice for sacrifice are chickens (regardless of color although some people insist the color of the chicken and the sex are determining factors as to whether or not they are fit to sacrifice) as sheep tend to be less common and used only occasionally. Why chickens and sheep? It's merely history that dictates the sacrifice used during a specific ritual. During the middle ages when many of the family grimoires were written, sheep and chickens flourished. They were plentiful and convenient. Nowadays, these animals have merely become a tradition. And, staying within the traditions of the religion, the sacrifices are consumed at a feast directly following the ritual. The Coven/Sects that do practice ritual sacrifice are not apt to do them more than once a year (usually during the Rite to Eurynomous ) if at all. Most modern ritual grimoires have exempted the sacrifice sections of ritual by snipping them as if they never existed at all.

The reasoning behind this is clear. Ritual sacrifice, even of a mere chicken, doesn't look good. With all the bad press surrounding left-hand-path religions already - modern Demonolators have chosen to keep some history buried deep in the pages of tattered grimoires locked in safes and collecting dust on bookshelves. What we fail to remember is that many other religions, including early Christian Sects, partook in sacrificial rites during the course of their history.

A popular question that often arises concerns the matter of a coven member leaving the coven or sect: It has been rumored far and wide that members who betrayed the coven were murdered, but not by physical means. Rather the coven would employ a curse to avenge justice on the offending person. However, this is not true. Members can leave the Coven/Sect at any time without fear of harm. Older grimoires such as the Willit and Delaney grimoires contain rites where a member is officially removed from the sect. The rites are somewhat similar to a marriage unbinding rite (formal divorce).

## The Composition of a Coven/Sect and Titles

The Demonolatry Sect is composed of three groups of people. Those who are students/initiates, those who are adepts, and those of the priesthood. It is the job of the

Student to study to become an adept. Once the student has taken the classes or training she becomes an Initiate. Once initiated she becomes an Apprentice. The next "rank" so to speak is the Adept. This is a person who knows enough to guide those still learning. Unless a person is born into a Demonolatry family, she may not ascend to the High Priesthood, however, she may become an Assistant Priest. Please note that birth into a Demonolatry family does not automatically give High Priesthood privileges. These people are required to ascend the levels just like everyone else. They just have an advantage in that most people born into Demonolatry families are Adept in their early teen years and Assisting Priests in their late teens and early twenties.

Since their families begin teaching them Demonolatry from day one - it just becomes something natural to them. If two Adepts marry and have a child, that child is eligible to someday preside as a High Priestess. It's just the way it is and always has been. However -- there are exception to any rule. Exceptions, though, are a rarity.

**The purpose of each title is as follows:**

**Student** - Someone still in the process of taking classes and learning basics.

**Initiate** - Can help students. Is officially initiated and dedicated to a patron Demon. Has passed all required classes. Knows basic rituals and practices them.

**Apprentice** - Can help Initiates and Students along. Has been taken under the wing of an Adept or member of the Priesthood to discover her talents and to use these talents during ritual for further spiritual dedication and fulfillment.

Begins to formulate her own rituals and to become more familiar with complex rituals. Is baptized if not already.

**Adept** - A practicing Demonolator who is knowledgeable to help Students-Apprentices. Can take on Apprentices. Is eligible to study to become an Assisting Priest.

**Assisting Priest** - Assists members of the priesthood during ritual. Has the authority to lead others in basic rituals. Has the authority to do initiations on a small scale.

**High Priest** - Guides all members of the Coven/Sect in spiritual matters, presides at all rituals although may stand aside and allow the Assisting to take over during basic rituals including initiations. The high priest(ess') are the only ones allowed to preside during mass initiations, baptismal rites, weddings, and funerals. The High Priest counsels members and offers help and guidance when needed.

Some sects will break down their titles to a degree system. In this instance, there are usually nine degrees, ten if you count the pre-initiate phase. Of the nine degrees, three are initiate degrees, three are adept degrees, and three are priesthood degrees. To learn more about the solitary practitioner and determining where you are, see the chapter *Moving Onward*. Also note that titles are a rite of passage indicating the individual has reached a defined state of spiritual growth.

## The Courtesies of the Sorcerer or Sect Law

Before we start getting into actual ritual work and the basics of Demonolatry Magick, I think it's important to take a moment to discuss Sect Law. Sect Law governs the behaviors of the Demonolator who practices magick in a group setting.

In my previous books I used Dukante's actual Courtesies as written by him. However, it was modified by Ellen Purswell in 2005, and quite frankly, I like her rendition of Sect Law better than Dukante's, perhaps because she used the word Magician instead of Sorcerer. So here are Mrs. Purswell's Courtesies of the Sorcerer, reprinted here with permission (first published in her book *Goetic Demonolatry*, DB Publishing 2005). In hers, she explains the reasoning behind each of the "laws".

· **The magician who hath a supposed greater knowledge of magick and contradicts knowledge of another magician of greater or lesser rank will never excel in his studies.** [*This basically means keep your ego in check. You are still only mortal and arrogance on your behalf will only hold you back.*]

· **The powerful magician doth not boast of power or greater knowledge. He shall excel.** [*A little humility goes a long way.*]

· **The rank of one magician compared to that of another should not be viewed as competition**. [*You are not in competition with others of your faith, you are brethren and should help one another.*]

· **A magician of lesser rank is not inferior and should not view another of greater rank as a threat, but as an equal and one to be learned from**. [*Those more experienced can help you achieve your goals.*]

· **A magician of greater rank is not superior and should not view another of lower rank as weak or inferior, but**

**as an equal and one to be learned from.** [*The experience of the magician should not be used to pull rank.*]

· **What one magician sees as the best or only way of magick, another may not. We are all individuals.** [*There are many ways to perform the same magickal operation and no one way is the best way. What works for one person may not work for another.*]

· **As in everything, each individual has an area within magick where he is most adept and will excel rapidly.** [*We all have different strengths and weaknesses. It's up to us to find out where we excel and where we could use practice. Know thyself.*]

· **Each magician is given at least one gift from the universe (Satan). This gift may be one that another magician might possess, but another will lack in to where excelling is almost impossible. This is because a gift is a natural extension of something the magician is born with.** [*Don't beat yourself up if divination comes easier to others than it does to you otherwise your self-confidence will duly suffer. You might pack a wallop when it comes to sending and directing energy whereas those who excel at divination might not.*]

If you are interested in practicing magick in conjunction with your Demonolatry practice (as many Demonolators do) then keep Sect Law in mind. Dukante said that those who did not follow Sect Law would have their natural gifts taken from them because the Demons have little patience with the Magician who uses his gifts foolishly.

# Proper Invocation, Tools, Ritual Execution and Layout

### The Basic Ritual Tools of the Demonolator

These are things you probably ought to acquire for your practice. These items are quite basic. The purpose each item serves is listed after the item.

**Sword**- For invocation. To invoke, the point of the blade faces skyward and you trace a D and a Z interwoven[6]. You can also use the sword to trace the circle on the ground. Look in sporting goods catalogs for inexpensive, suitable swords.

**Dagger** – For invocation. I actually prefer the dagger for invocation because a sword can be clumsy. Also for dispersal of water if needed and for drawing blood. Though for blood drawing, a diabetic pen with disposable lancets is safest and most sanitary, especially in a group. Again, look

---

[6] See invocation section for diagram.

in sporting goods catalogs. They often sale sharp, inexpensive daggers suitable for ritual.

**Chalice** - For water or drink. It's probably safe to have two or three. Try thrift stores or pawn shops.

**Bowl** - For burning requests and incense during ritual. Must be able to withstand heat. You will need two bowls. Once again, thrift stores and antique shops tend to have the best selection.

**Candle Holders** - Buy various sizes. Also make sure they suit your personality. Thrift stores and antique shops will also be able to help you out here.

**Assorted Candles** - Various colors and sizes. Larger candles will serve as altar candles while tapers will serve as focus or purpose candles. Also consider elemental point candles. The best place to buy is a hobby/craft store. Candles are often less expensive there.

**Assorted Oleums and Incenses** - For use during ritual. Start with basic sets and work into well defined Oleums and Incenses as needed.

**The Cord of Nine /Prayer Cords** - This is an item notoriously used in medieval grimoires (black books) for cursing. It is also known as the witches ladder. This is a piece of leather or rope in which nine knots are tied. Each knot represents one of the nine Demonic divinities. The first five are the five elements being Lucifer, Flereous, Leviathan, Belial, and Satan. The next two are the positive and negative polarities being Amducious for destruction and Verrine for healing. The last two are life, Unsere, and death, Eurynomous. The cord is used during devotional prayer and religious rites.

Prayer cords can be of any color and can be created with the Nine Divinities in any order you choose.

Traditionally the Demonic Divinities fall in the following order with regard to basic prayer cords:

1. Satan
2. Lucifer
3. Flereous
4. Leviathan
5. Belial
6. Unsere
7. Amducious
8. Verrine
9. Eurynomous

The prayer cords are used during, well, prayer. As you run your thumb and forefinger over each knot, you say a prayer to the divinity that knot represents. Prayer cords are older than Christianity and were the inspiration for Catholic rosary beads.

Each of your tools should be consecrated and cleaned elementally. While cleaning them you should stay clear of chemical abrasives. Use a dagger and hot water to remove melted wax. Use earth to scour, fire to sterilize, water for rinsing, and let everything air dry. You might want to dry any silver so it doesn't tarnish or get water spots. All ritual tools should be cleaned at least once a year whether they are in need of it or not. There are formal consecration rituals in which the patron/matron Demon is called on to bless each item. However, these types of rituals can be done during larger rites, and therefore I have not included a formal ritual here.

## The Powers that Be

According to Richard Dukanté[7] there were 13 powers that suggested the level a practitioner of Demonolatry was working at. He defined them as such:

1. The ability to forget what is known and useless. Consistent and spontaneous workings.

2. Recognition, balance, and working with each element/Demon harmoniously.

3. The gathering and projection of the will.

4. The difference between common sense and knowledge.

5. Realization of ones own limits and omitting the effects of power upon the practitioner. [i.e. ego trips and the like]

6. The defined laws of sorcery are the courtesies.

7. Maintaining alpha through a working of ritual magick at will.

8 The recognition of one's own power phases corresponding to hours, days, and planets.

9. Specific precision and will.

10. Interpretation of formulas and ritual workings.

11. Transcendence to a higher magick.

12. Invitation to physical manifestations at will.

---

[7] Book 3, page 67.

13. Ascending to the Demonic plane.

## A Word About Languages

Latin, Hebrew, and French are the most commonly used languages in older grimoires. Why? First, not all grimoire authors were English speaking people. Also, (this is especially true for Latin text) back when education was privialge, whatever information hid itself among the pages of old grimoires was secret only to those without education making magickal practice in all forms an educated man's luxury.

Nowadays, if a student wishes to study the older texts in order that she may understand ritual magick further, she must learn something of the above languages. It is recommended that you have a Latin dictionary, a Hebrew dictionary, and a French dictionary. The reasoning behind this is that you will, over time, familiarize yourself with the different languages and be able to recognize them. While not everyone is destined to be able to speak these languages fluently, basic familiarity and dictionaries can help with translation.

## Ritual Music

Ritual music is a wonderful way to invoke atmosphere, which in turn can help the mental focus of the Demonolator who meditates in prayer as well as the Demonolator who practices ritual magick. For Coven/Sects the preference tends to lean toward traditional hymns and chants. Solitary Demonolators, however, have reported finding solace in every type of music from Celtic Classical to Death Metal. Others still find ritual music to detract from the practitioner/worshipper's concentration and choose silence instead. Ritual music is really a personal preference.

To find your personal preference try rites with and without different types of music. You may find that certain rituals are empowered with music while others seem sapped of their energy with it.

The altarnative is to chant the Demonic Enns. Using a monotone, rhythmic tone to chant the Enn, the Enn is usually chanted until the participants of the ritual feel enough energy has been built or until the High Priest(ess) indicates the energy level has reached its optimum.

Perhaps one of the more popular chanted hymns is "Melus De Quo Magna". It is versatile in that it can be used in any ritual for any purpose. It is merely a statement that all things come from the Demonic elements. It is, however, not as appropriate for highly religious rites such as Baphometic Fire Baptisms, Weddings, or Funerals since the practice of ritual magick is not performed during these rites. Different Coven/Sects have different preferences with regard to hymns and chanting.

You can get these hymns on CD (*Abyss: Daemonolatry Hymns for Ritual and Meditation*) from DB Publishing. You can also find the hymns in the back of this book. For reference, here are the words to *Melus De Quo Magna*.

Prodere foras
quo numen de magicus
ad- mihi ejus
neus veneficium.

**Translation:** Outside in nature, there is magic in everything, provided by the divine powers for use in the workings of sorcery.

## Basic Altar Set-Up

There are two altar candles. One on either side of the altar. They serve the purpose of light since candles will be your sole light source. For outdoor rituals, tiki-torches are wonderful. On the center of the altar is what is called the *focus candle*. It symbolizes the power and focus point of the rite. Traditionally this candle is thick and pillar-like and usually purple or black. Surrounding the center candle are the purpose candles used to focus for secondary rite purposes. In front of that is the incense bowl and burning bowl for requests. For sect rites some people choose to place the burning bowl in front of the altar at its own table. All daggers and swords are placed on the right of the altar while all chalices, incenses, parchment, writing instruments (a cheap Schaefer fountain pen works wonderfully), and all other needed items hail to your left. This is a very simple set up and can be modified to be as elaborate or simple as you prefer. For group rites, consider setting up "stations". One station is for blood drawing, one for requests, one for anointing, and so on.

## Basic Ritual Execution

Ritual consists of three universal parts true to all schools of occult thought. The Beginning/Opening, The Middle, and The End/Closing.

**THE BEGINNING** - The invocation/invitation of the entity you are calling to draw power from or the entities meant to protect you. In Demonolatry, an elemental circle is invoked with the Demons Belial for North/Earth, Lucifer for East/Air, Flereous for South/Fire, and Leviathan for West/Water. Satan can also be invited as the fifth element, or the wellspring from which all energy flows. Note that some occult schools of thought call the fifth element spirit.

The proper invocations for each of the elements is as follows:

- To Invoke Earth: "Lirach Tasa Vefa Wehlic, Belial."
- To Invoke Air: "Renich Tasa Uberaca Biasa Icar, Lucifer."
- To Invoke Fire: "Ganic Tasa fubin, Flereous."
- To Invoke Water: "Jedan Tasa hoet naca, Leviathan."
- For Satan - Tasa reme laris Satan - Ave Satanis

For rites of nine (see appropriate section), you would invoke all nine divinities.

Remember that evocation suggests calling a Demon to physical manifestation against his will while invocation is a prayer asking the Demon to be present or to bless the rite.

**NOTE:** Just in case you missed it, a word about the Demonic Enns or Invocations. No one knows what language the Enns come from. They were deemed Demonic Enns in late 16th Century (1585) by Demonolator Alexander Willit[8].

**THE MIDDLE** - The middle is literally the "Definition" of the ritual's purpose. This is the part where you invoke/invite the Demon for this purpose. It is the body of the ritual. It is where the actual "working" of magick and worship takes place. Anything can happen amidst the not-so-rigid confines of the ritual body.

**THE END** - Here you dismiss/say good-bye to the Demons you've invoked/invited usually with a polite "We thank

---

[8] From the Willit Family Grimoire circa 1648.

thee [Demon's name]. Go in peace." Candles are extinguished. Clean up and so on.

For **Magickal practice** we can break this down even further into three aspects of ritual.

The **symbolic aspects** of magickal practice.

- Ritual Space
- Ritual Tools
- Amulets, Talismans, and Sigils

The **spiritual and belief aspects** of magickal practice.

- Personal Pantheons/Demons
- Prayer and Invocation
- Basic Belief

The **purposeful aspects** of magickal practice.

- Spells
- Rituals

The ritual (magickal *or* spiritual) can be further broken down into seven parts.

- Define the ritual's purpose and desired outcome.
- Create or gather the invocations.
- Outline the steps of the ritual:
    o Beginning - invocations
    o Middle – the work
    o End - closing

- Assemble the proper sigils, herbal mixtures, and/or magickal items.
- Prepare the ritual chamber and yourself.
- Perform the ritual.
- Post-ritual follow-up.

## Define the Purpose and Desired Outcome:

The first step to creating any effective ritual is to define your purpose. Be as specific as you can be. "I need some extra cash" is pretty vague but sometimes a necessary way of putting it. "I want my boss to give me a raise" is more specific. "I want to get a better job" is pretty vague, too. Try adding the field you'd like to work in (be realistic) to that sentence. "I'd like to get a better engineering job" is more specific.

Sometimes being specific is impractical. In cases like that, feel free to define your rituals' purpose and desired goal in broad, sweeping statements. However, being specific has its advantages. First, it helps you focus more clearly on the desired outcome. Second, it gives you a clearer picture of what it is that you really want. Do you really want a raise, or a new job? Don't heehaw around.

Some rites have no other purpose than to honor the Demons. If that is the case – then this is the purpose and desired outcome.

## Create or gather the Invocations

Next, decide which member(s) of your personal pantheon is/are appropriate to the ritual's purpose and gather or create (if you do not have an Enn) the invocations necessary. For this particular working (to get a raise) I would choose Belphegore. An example (continuing along the lines of wanting a raise) of a created invocation might go something like this:

*"Belphegore, of earth, please attend this rite. I call upon you with an offering. Hear me; be present at this rite to bring good fortune to me.*

You can then add another invocation during the body of the ritual (where the work is performed) that better defines the purpose and goal of your ritual to the Demons you are calling upon. That might go something like this:

*"Belphegore, of earth, I ask that you grant me the strength to find stability at my job, and the earthly skills to excel there, so that I might get a raise in pay."*

While these examples may not be as eloquent as you might choose to write your own invocations, they illustrate how specific the invocations should be. The more specific the invocation, the more you understand what you really want, and the Demons are better able to help you and you are better able to honor them. Asking the external forces to simply *get you a raise* probably isn't going to be as effective. Keep in mind any colors, symbols, or correspondences you will need to follow to make your *guests* comfortable.

## Outline the Steps of the Ritual

Next you will want to outline the steps of the ritual. This can be as simple as writing down your invocations for the beginning and middle, and writing down your *"thank you, please depart and drive safely"* for the closing. This means that anything during the body of the ritual (the middle) is fair game. If you would like to perform spells or symbolic action during the work, pray, sing, dance, paint, cook, eat – or whatever it is you do during the body of your rituals – you can note it if you are worried about forgetting a specific part.

Otherwise, during the middle of the ritual you can do whatever you feel like doing in the present moment. With rites like this, make sure you have everything you could possibly want within your circle including parchment, candles, ink, oils, incenses, paints, canvas, music, cooking utensils etc…

I know it may sound strange to have some of these items within a ritual circle, but you must always remember that whatever you are doing during the body of the rite it must have personal meaning to you, it must connect you to your personal pantheon, and it must be done with the purpose and the desired outcome of the ritual in mind.

If you feel like writing a script, do it. If prepared scripts seem to hamper the flow of the ritual, don't use them. As you are planning the working part of your ritual, be sure to note any colors, sigils, or correspondence you want to use during the ritual. You might also want to plan a time for the ritual based on moon phase, hour, etc…

Keep in mind that sigils and talismans can be made during the body of the ritual if you prefer to construct them within a ritual circle.

The closing of the ritual can be elaborate or as simple as you wish. In the case of Belphegore I might say something like,

*"Belphegore, of earth, thank you for attending this rite. Go in peace."*

Basically you are telling your assembled guests (your personal pantheon) that you appreciate them coming over to help, and you are seeing them to the door like you might a houseguest.

**Assemble the proper sigils, herbal mixtures, and/or magickal items.**

Nothing is more frustrating than to have constructed a ritual circle only to find you've forgotten something. Make yourself a list of all the things you want and take them to the ritual chamber or space beforehand. That way nothing is left behind.

**Prepare the Ritual Chamber and Yourself**

Think of this as set up. Some people, during the planning stage, like to draw diagrams of the ritual's layout. Use this technique if it helps you. Having the ritual space set up ahead of time will free you up to prepare yourself.

Some people may wish to bathe in ritual salts or oils. Others may choose to fast before the ritual. Others still may choose to take their time putting on their robes and mentally preparing themselves for a ritual. Perhaps you want to do all three. Those choices are entirely up to you.

**Perform the Ritual**

I don't think I need to go further into this. But make sure you've set enough time aside to perform the ritual. Especially if you are on borrowed private time and your roommate will be home in an hour.

## Post Ritual Follow-Up

After doing a ritual working of magick, you can't just sit idly by and wait for a raise or new job to fall in your lap. Nor should you go to work and cuss your boss, or sit at home expecting the phone to ring with a better job offer. Instead, you have to actively participate in magick. That participation means getting to work on time and showing your boss you are competent and deserving of a raise. It means you have to go out and fill out applications.

## The Purpose of the Circle

A circle is created not to bind the Demons, but rather to balance the energies they bring to the ritual. There are other types of rites that employ triangles where all nine divinities are called upon (three to each point). These rites exist to create a more vibrant flow of energy. I warn new practitioners to stay away from triangle, or pyramid rites as we call them, at first because the energy can be strong, overwhelming, and deeply unsettling for those who have not experienced imbalanced Demonic presence. They can even be unsettling for the adept and can cause nausea, vomiting, dizziness, and in rare cases – fainting. So before working a pyramid rite, drink plenty of fluids (even if fasting) and be aware that rites employing a triangle produce strong, imbalanced energy and an elemental balancing rite may be necessary afterward.

**Proper Invocation Techniques**

When calling the Demons into your ritual circle, the traditional way to do it is to use the Enn, or an invocation of your own devise, and use the ritual dagger or your hand to draw the following in the air in front of you (kinda diagonal to the sky if that makes sense), starting at the arrow and ending at the dot:

It starts with the point closest to the arrow with Unsere, next is Lucifer, next is Flereous, next is Verrine, next is Belial, then Amducious, then Leviathan, Satan, and finally it ends at the dot with Eurynomous. It starts with creation, moves to enlightenment, and ends with destruction. It repeats this cycle three times.

Now for a few definitions. I've recently learned that Ceremonial and Goetic Magician's use their own definitions of invoke and evoke. I was told that **to Ceremonial Magicians, evoke is the external**

**manifestation and invoke is the internal manifestation** (which they also sometimes call possession, which is also strange, but it's their lingo).

It drives me nuts because that is not what those words mean according to the dictionary, but I totally respect the Ceremonial Magician's specialized definitions and their right to use them. After all, I have no issue with evocation used to bring parts of the psyche to the forefront for "Self" work, which is really how most CM's see Demons (as negative/evil aspects of the human psyche, so to speak, as opposed to actual neutral entities).

It's just that Demonolators use the dictionary definitions for these same words - not the CM definitions. If you're unsure, just look in a dictionary.

**Invocation-** The act of calling on (a higher power) for assistance, support, or inspiration.

*CM's say this is the internal, but by definition this would technically be external because the actual definition suggests a power outside the self. However, since we are each a part of the divine and all that is I can see where they get their "internal" definition.* Invocation is what we Demonolators do.

**We do not evoke Demons under any circumstance**.

**Evocation** - The act of summoning (like you might a servant or subordinate) an entity (implied: against its will. Also implied: Demons are servants.)

*CM's say this is the external, but by definition the implication of evoke is both internal and external and suggests something the magician creates from or evokes from himself or forces from another source.*

**NOTE: Demonolators find evocation VERY disrespectful.**

Now, I'd like to discuss another aspect. That of possession vs. channeling. Demonolators are never Possessed by Demons. Possession, by its very definition means against the individual's will. Demonolators believe that Demons have no need for possession.

**Possessed** - Controlled (implied against one's will) by a spirit or other force.

*CM's have often used this word in front of me to describe what Demonolators would call channeling. Possession means the magician has no will to stop it and the wording of the definition implies the same.*

We do, however, believe in Channeling Demons. There are methods to do this.

**Channeling** - The medium through which a spirit-guide purportedly communicates with the physical world. (This is with the person's consent because they have to physically open themselves up for the experience.)

*CM's don't seem to use this word.*

# Dedication and Initiation

## How the Practitioner Chooses The Counterpart Demon

Choosing your counterpart Demon (Matron/Patron) can be an interesting experience. It requires honesty of the Self and some know how of the occult for it to be successful. Yes, you can end up choosing a counterpart unsuccessfully. However, you mustn't worry. Unsuccessful choices usually result in partial imbalances that are easily corrected.

You should choose a Demon that closely resembles some aspect of you. **EXAMPLE:** If you are a bookworm or love to learn then your obvious choice for a counterpart would be Ronwe, the Demon of knowledge. You should research your Demon in full to make sure this is truly the Demon you wish to be your counterpart. If you'd rather not choose your Demon in this manner, a choice that is always available is your elemental Demon.

The simplest of ways of choosing your Demon is to know your element. You can base your element on a natal chart, a sun sign, or how you generally feel. Throughout the book I will use the Dukanté Hierarchy as a model to illustrate methods.

Perhaps you are a Sagittarius (fire) with Taurus (earth) rising, but you generally feel watery due to your deep emotions and innate creativity. You can choose Flereous, Belial, or Leviathan for your counterpart. To sum it up nicely - you could not go wrong with Flereous, Leviathan might work adequately, but Belial probably isn't the best choice. Now if you often felt earthy then Flereous and Belial would both become viable choices. See below.

Note that Elemental counterparts go hand-in-hand with elemental Magick. This may be the route to go especially if you have a background in elemental Magick. By now you are probably seeing how personalized this can become.

| Sun Sign | Element | Ruling Planet | Elemental Demon |
|----------|---------|---------------|-----------------|
| Aquarius | Air | Uranus | Lucifer |
| Aries | Fire | Mars | Flereous |
| Cancer | Water | Moon | Leviathan |
| Capricorn | Earth | Saturn | Belial |
| Gemini | Air | Mercury | Lucifer |
| Leo | Fire | Sun | Flereous |
| Libra | Air | Venus | Lucifer |
| Pisces | Water | Neptune | Leviathan |
| Sagittarius | Fire | Jupiter | Flereous |
| Scorpio | Water | Mars | Leviathan |
| Taurus | Earth | Venus | Belial |
| Virgo | Earth | Mercury | Belial |

## The Self-Dedication Ritual:

**Take your time choosing a Demon to dedicate yourself to. There is no hurry.**

When it is supposed to happen, it will. It is suggested you work with many Demons before you take that step toward dedication. You can practice Demonolatry for years without being dedicated to a particular Demon. It just so happens that after time, many Demonolators may find they are more connected or drawn to one particular Demon over the others. This Rite basically acknowledges and strengthens that bond.

### Will I notice a change right away after doing a dedication?

Probably not. But don't worry. A dedication is not the solve-all to all our earthly problems. A dedication is a rite that solidifies a bond between your Self and a Demon. It doesn't mean that the Demon is going to start talking to you all the time or manifest around every corner. Instead, your Matron/Patron is your primary guide. No doubt you will find other Demons are stronger along your path. That's because you might need help from a different Demon at a particular time in your life. In instances like this the Matron/Patron will step aside to allow that other Demon to step forward to offer its guidance.

### Then why choose a Matron/Patron at all?

A Matron/Patron is a counterpart to balance the individual. It is in this balance that we can see things clearer and begin to know the Self, better.

## Patrons/Matrons and Mentors

There is a difference between patrons/matrons and mentor Demons. Patrons (masculine) or Matrons (feminine) have a bond with the practitioner that's always strong. They are naturally attracting to one another.

Mentors, however, come to the practitioner unbidden and may show interest in "mentoring" the Demonolator through a specific life phase or situation in which (s)he needs help and the Demon has lessons to impart. When Mentors show up, the Matron/Patron often steps aside. This is normal and required so that the Mentor can help you as much as possible. Once you no longer need the Mentor, the Patron/Matron steps back to take the Mentor's place.

A practitioner can find him or herself under a mentor for years at a time. Oftentimes, the practitioner becomes concerned that the bond with the Matron/Patron has been lost, or worries (s)he chose the wrong Demon to dedicate him or herself to. This is not the case. The M/Patron will always return, as does the close relationship. The relationship with the mentor can also become close. In your lifetime, you could have numerous mentors come to you depending on what the Demons think you need and what you think you need. There is no dedication done to a mentor.

Dedication rituals should be done on a day of importance to you if at all possible. Birthdays, children's birthdays, or dates holding some significance to you are ideal. If you cannot wait for this date you can use a new or full moon in its place or use planetary charts to plan your ritual. See planning section below. You will need to gather the following items:

Bell or Gong, 2 Chalices, Pure Solar Sea Salt, water from a running river, a bowl for incense, an iron cast bowl/urn for burning, an athame' or dagger, a sword for invocation, parchment, ink, an appropriate incense for your element.

You will need to know: The Demon you plan to dedicate yourself to as a counterpart, your element, and the place your ritual will commence. The incense bases for each element are as follows:

Water - Calamus Base
Earth - Patchouli Base
Air - Wormwood Base
Fire - Sandalwood Base.

**Preparation for the Ritual:**

Plan ahead of time. You should allow yourself at least 3 days preparation. If you smoke, drink, or use recreational drugs you must refrain from doing so for at least 48 hours before performing this ritual. You must also fast 24 hours, drinking plenty of liquids, unless you have a medical condition that does not allow you to do so. Sexual intercourse should also be avoided during this time since it drains physical energy. Make sure your items have all been acquired, that you have chosen your counterpart Demon, and that you have chosen a ritual place where you will not be disturbed.

**The Ritual:**

This ritual may be done skyclad (naked) or robed. Use an invitation/conjuration to your liking to gather the elements at their compass points of your ritual circle.

- To Invoke Earth: Lirach Tasa Vefa Wehlic, Belial.
- To Invoke Air: Renich Tasa Uberaca Biasa Icar, Lucifer.
- To Invoke Fire: Ganic Tasa fubin, Flereous.
- To Invoke Water: Jedan Tasa hoet naca, Leviathan.

Once you have called the elements and your circle has been constructed- write on a piece of paper:

*I, [your name], do hereby dedicate myself unto [Demon's name]. By Satan - the infernal monarch and ruler of the elements - I do swear allegiance to [Demon name] forever hereafter. I will serve and work with you as you so ask. Accept me now as a dedicated student to the element of your design. I affix my seal below.*

Sign dedication.

Meditate in your devotion for no less than one half hour. Once you feel the presence of your chosen Demon (and you will feel it) - burn the dedication. Close the ritual.

**The Aftermath:**

This ritual requires no further maintenance save you remain dedicated as you have promised. Once you have dedicated yourself to a Demon, you cannot dedicate yourself to another. This is why it is so important to be sure about your choice. Failure to remain dedicated is between you and your chosen entity. Some people have reported nothing adverse has happened while others say they have had nothing but ill befall them. I believe this has to do with the perception of the worshiper, and whether or not they feel guilt more deeply. Remember, Demons are peculiar entities who have particular likes, dislikes, and temperaments. The more you work with a Demon, the more you will understand the Demon's temperament.

## The Initiation -

The initiation into Demonolatry can happen one of two ways. Through self-dedication and self-initiation, or through self-dedication and sect initiation. Some sects require you to be baptized before being initiated. Others will allow baptism at a later date. Either way, you will likely have to study for some time before being initiated.

The basic initiation rite is as follows: The ritual begins by the basic construction of an elemental circle. The initiate enters at the North part of the ritual chamber as North signifies new beginnings in Demonolatry. At each elemental point the initiate is presented by the priest or priestess to the elemental Demon as such: [Demon Name], we present you [Initiate's Name] - a true follower of your path. Grant him/her the wisdom to know your divine power.

The Initiate Responds at each Element thus: Hail [Demon's Name].

Coven/Sect follows with resounding "Hail"

The initiate must then kneel before the altar and cut her hand, allowing her blood to spill into the chalice in which the blood of the rest of the coven has been placed. Once mixed with water blessed by the Demon Leviathan, the initiate is presented to the Coven/Sects patron Demon. This can vary from Sect to Sect. Once this is done, the initiate is asked to drink from the chalice. The chalice is then passed from member to member. Some coven/sects give the initiate a name which the Demons will know him/her by and/or a pendant to wear signifying their acceptance into the group. But usually, the giving of the Demonic name is saved for the Adepthood rite.

For self-initiation, the rite proceeds likewise except the initiate must present him/herself : [Demon Name], I present myself to you as a true follower of your path. Grant me the wisdom to know your divine power. Hail [Demon Name]. The initiate must them present herself at the altar and must cut her hand letting blood fall into the chalice. The initiate mixes the blood with water, presents it to Leviathan: "Leviathan - bless this water that I may cleanse myself and start my life anew as a Demonolator." Once this is done the initiate presents herself to the patron Demon or Satan. She then drinks from the chalice.

A pre-purified pendant of significance can be made for the purpose of this ritual so that when the initiate finishes the self-initiation she can give herself the pendant. The pendant is merely a reminder and a symbol of faith, love and devotion.

Self-dedications can be done before or after a sect or self initiation.

**The difference between a baptism, an initiation, and a dedication:**

Baptism = Starting your life over as a Demonolator. Or beginning your life as a Demonolator, whichever is appropriate.

Dedication = Allegiance and bonding to a specific Demon entity.

Initiation = A rite welcoming a new person into a Coven/Sect, or the practice of Demonolatry in general.

**Demonolatry Holidays:**

| Month/Day | Holiday |
| --- | --- |
| March 21 | Equinox Rite to Lucifer |
| April 30 | Walpurgisnacht/May Eve - Initiations and first Rite to Leviathan |
| June 22 | Solstice Rite to Flereous |
| September 21 | Equinox Rite to Leviathan |
| October 31 | All Hallows Eve/Halloween Rite to Eurynomous & Baalberith |
| December 22 | Solstice Rite to Belial |

While Solstices and Equinox's celebrate the changing of seasons and the Demonic elements, May Eve is the second rite to Leviathan. Sometimes, the May ritual is not held until the first or second of May. This is a ritual where new initiates are presented to their new Sects. The October 31 rite is a rite to Eurynomous, Balberith, and Babael. The death Demons of the [9]fifth family. There is also a second rite to Lucifer done in mid-November. However, for unknown reasons, the second rite to Lucifer was abandoned by many Demonolatry sects in the 19th century. It has recently been re-introduced.

---

[9] The Fifth Family Referring to the Dukanté Grimoire Hierarchy.

# Prayer

Unfortunately, when many people look at prayer, they think of the Christianized version - groveling before deity begging for mercy. Some people may also see prayer as a way to get stuff as in, "Dear God, please give me a new car." In truth, prayer is neither of these things.

**Prayer is defined as**, *"A reverent petition made to God, a god, or another object of worship. An act of communion with God, a god, or another object of worship, such as in devotion, confession, praise, or thanksgiving."*

## As in reverent petitions the following are appropriate:

*"Lord Leviathan, please grant me the emotional strength and control to not strangle my annoying co-worker. I thank you for this. Amen."*

*"Lord Belphegore, please help me find the insight to a new opportunity to make additional income. I thank you for this. Amen."*

## The following are simply ridiculous:

*"Lord Rosier, make Martha love me and want to jump my bones!"*

*"Lord Satan, let me win the lottery!"*

## Reverence is defined as:

1. A feeling of profound awe and respect and often love; veneration.
2. An act showing respect, especially a bow or curtsy.
3. The state of being revered.

Basically this means that praying to ask for strength, insight, wisdom, and such things are fine as they are reverent to the Demon. You are seeking their wisdom and energies to help you. In the latter examples, the petitioner was asking for impossible things, using the Demons as if they were genies granting wishes. This is where the old Arabic mythologies of the jinn (djinn) come in, and Solomon's work with the Goetic hierarchy.

But what about magickal workings where you are seeking Martha's love or you want to win the lottery? ***Realistic*** is the key word here. You can pray and ask Verrine to help heal a sick friend, or you can ask Verrine to grant your friend strength to heal herself. The latter is more realistic because the Demons are known to help those who help themselves. They will rarely hand you anything, especially if you have the power to change things on your own. That is one of the many lessons Demons often impart to their followers. Do for yourself, and seek the Demons for strength and guidance to help you reach your goals. Do not seek them to hand you stuff. It isn't likely to happen.

Oftentimes, prayer is in thanksgiving. We often forget that the lessons the Demons teach us are things to be thankful for. When I first started practicing Demonolatry years ago, I was a shy girl and did not stand up for myself. Through my practice of Demonolatry and lessons I've been taught through Demonic intervention, I learned not only how to stand up for myself, but how to interact with people better. I thank the Demons daily for helping me to achieve that strength. Notice how I do not give them all the credit.

The divine can only do so much on its own. We exist as the physical manifestation of the divine. That said, we are part of the divine just as the Demons are. This brings me to my next point – prayer can also be a petition to this Divine part of the Self. The Demons won't be upset. You should treat yourself as you treat them and give yourself credit when you achieve something with Demonic influence or without. Give the credit where credit is due. It doesn't make you egotistical. It simply strengthens self-deification through which you better understand your higher Self. To know thyself is the key to living the life you want, here and now.

Prayer can also be relayed in an offering of respect and reverence. You can offer sigils to the flame in prayer. You can offer incenses, oleums, blood, and even strong emotions of excitement, happiness, love and devotion.

Prayer works by a positive exchange of energy. You offer the Demon positive energy and reverence during prayer and that energy is returned from the Demon, to you, as even stronger energy. This is why praying works and has not been abandoned. It also offers a communion between the individual and deity. A direct link or bond that, when cultivated, grows into a strong connection with the divine intelligences we call Demons and all that is - Satan.

Let us dissect a prayer for a moment. The prayer can be broken down into four parts.

1.  Acknowledgement
2.  Reverent Petition or Offering
3.  Thanksgiving
4.  Sending the prayer

**The Acknowledgement**
*"Lord Leviathan,*

**The Reverent Petition or Offering**
*please grant me the emotional strength and control to not strangle my annoying co-worker.*

**Thanksgiving**
*I thank you for this,*

**Sending the Prayer**
*Amen."*

Not all four parts are always present in words, but they should be present in thought and feeling.

But Amen is a Christian thing… Wrong. Amen is not a Christian exclusive ending to prayer. It comes from ancient Egypt from the deity Amen-Ra. As Amen, he was a hidden, secret God. Ra represented His tangible side. Amen was said at the end of prayer to send the prayer to the highest, most hidden God, Amen-Ra. So in this sense, you would literally be sending the prayer to the highest unseen power in the universe, Satan. Some people see Atem, Amen, and Satan as merely different aspects of the same deity. If you feel more comfortable, end each prayer with *Satan*. The concept is still the same. Some prayers are ended with Naamah as a blessing, as well. Saying Naamah is basically wishing a pleasant outcome, experience or journey. Used to bless items or people, Naamah means you are wishing the individual a pleasant experience or journey, or that the item blessed brings pleasure to the bearer or (as in the case of amulets) keeps their experiences pleasant or protected from discord. Keep this option in mind, too. How you end your prayers is up to you.

Prayer can even be unspoken. Prayer can take shape of an offering as well as long as all four parts of prayer are present in your thoughts and feelings as you are constructing the offering and giving it.

## Devotional Prayers and Meditations

### To Lucifer

It is our Lord Lucifer who hath brought us from the darkness into the light. He brightens our path so that we may find enlightenment. We honor him. His winds carry with them the promise of lessons learned for this lifetime. Hail Lucifer. Lord of Air.

### To Flereous

The fire rebirths us, and as the phoenix we, too, shall rise. Our Lord Flereous commands it so. From him we are blessed with our passions and loves. Our desires and energies. For all these things are Flereous. He brings to us action and desire giving our life's purpose vigor and strength. Hail our Lord Flereous. Lord of Fire.

## To Leviathan

We are cleansed in the waves of the ocean, our Lord Leviathan. For you give us the powers of intuition and emotion that guide our spiritual path. In your wisdom, as the serpent implies, you bring us faith and devotion and love. Your grace is everlasting and true and we are truly blessed. Hail our Lord Leviathan. Lord of Water.

## To Belial

Lord Belial brings us stability and knowledge. He is the strength of education and the pillar of senses. Through him we are encouraged to explore the world through sensation and pleasure. We are asked to discover. For this we have been truly blessed. Hail our Lord Belial. Lord of Earth.

# Death

### Funeral Oration

In darkness there comes a ray of light in the promise of rebirth foretold by our dark Lords. Hail Eurynomous and Baalberith. May Babael keep this burial place sacred and unsoiled. I pray you Lord Eurynomous for my loved ones safe passage to Unsere who brings life from the desolate.

## Devotional/Prayer

My darkest of Lords, hear me. For when I am dead you must know that I was faithful to you in life that I may greet you in respect, and that you may know me by name in death. Hail unto you and pray keep me safe until my time to leave this plane has come.

## Death of a Child

Lord Baalberith, please watch over this little child. (S)he has come to you in death. As protector of souls comfort and guide her to her resting place. May Babael guard her that no harm shall befall her. A life so young forsaken. We weep and find comfort in knowing she is now, and ever shall be among kindred. As her energy was in life so it returns to its source. Blessed are the children for their innocence. Blessed is this child. Lord Eurynomous protect and keep her, so be it.

## Death of a Pet

Even though this mere creature of Belial was not a man nor woman, (s)he was my friend and companion in life. Now, our Lord Eurynomous has taken her soul in peaceful rest. Thus we lay her to the ground, to the earth from whence she came. In sorrow we release her and in joy do we celebrate the dawn of her passing. Blessed are the beasts for their love in unconditional. Blessed are the beasts for their judgment lyes in truth. Protect and keep her, so be it.

# Devotions to the Nine Demonic Divinities

## Satan
Lord Satan, hear me. Blessed in your name I pray please keep me safe. Henceforth I vow my everlasting devotion and love. So be it.

## Belial
Lord Belial, hear me. Blessed in your name, I pray please keep me safe. Henceforth I vow my everlasting devotion and love. So be it.

## Lucifer
Lord Lucifer, hear me. Blessed in your name, I pray please keep me safe. Henceforth I vow my everlasting devotion and love. So be it.

## Flereous
Lord Flereous, hear me. Blessed in your name, I pray please keep me safe. Henceforth I vow my everlasting devotion and love. So be it.

## Leviathan
Lord Leviathan, hear me. Blessed in your name, I pray please keep me safe. Henceforth I vow my everlasting devotion and love. So be it.

## Unsere
Unsere, hear me. Blessed in your name, I pray please keep me safe. Henceforth I vow my everlasting devotion and love. So be it.

## Eurynomous
Lord Eurynomous, hear me. Blessed in your name, I pray please keep me safe. Henceforth I vow my everlasting devotion and love. So be it.

**Verrine**
Lord Verrine, hear me. Blessed in your name, I pray please keep me safe. Henceforth I vow my everlasting devotion and love. So be it.

**Amducious**
Lord Amduscius, hear me. Blessed in your name, I pray please keep me safe. Henceforth I vow my everlasting devotion and love. So be it.

# Introduction To Demonolatry Lessons for Pre-Initiates

This section is offered for Students of Demonolatry who are seeking initiation. Now that you have gotten this far and you understand the basics of Demonolatry, review what you have learned and do the assignments. If you have a teacher you are working with, turn your assignments in to him/her. If you do not have a teacher, doing the assignments for your own edification will help you absorb the material better.

These lessons may also be of benefit to adepts and those already initiated, as they contain supplemental material to the information already presented in this book.

The pre-initiate should keep a notebook in which to write journal entries and notes on the material.

**Notes For Adepts and Priesthood:** It can sometimes be helpful for students to give them due dates for each assignment. You might also have them turn in their notebooks once a week, or give them additional homework assignments as you see fit.

# LESSON ONE

For the best results - read through the class notes, note any questions you have, research your questions in this book, then contact your teacher with any questions that have not been answered. If there is any homework, you should do it and write a short journal entry or essay detailing your results. This should be turned into your teacher.

This first class is about the study of Demons, the nature of Demons and deity, and the worship of Demons as deities. The word Demon (from the Latin and Greek) originally meant a divine intelligence replete with wisdom. Divine comes from the Latin divus meaning God. Therefore, we can safely say that Demons did not start out as the Christian devils as the word now applies in our modern age. Demons were originally Gods in their own right.

First let's start by discussing Demonology, which is the study of Demons. Demonology as a study was created by the Christian church to catalogue Gods (aka Demons) of past religions. Perhaps the most notable are the 72 spirits of Solomon. These Goetic Demons date back to around 100 A.D. when the practice of Demonology and Demonography became common place among clergy of the Catholic church. Hebraic and other Demons were later catalogued by such noted Demonologists as Johan Weyer, Peter Binsfield, Pope Honorius, and so on. In most instances, these men took existing Demonic hierarchies and modified them, added to them, and changed them to create new hierarchies. It's no wonder that the history of many Demons has been lost through the passage of time. Dagon, for example, was allegedly a God of harvest before somehow finding a home as a serpent God of the underworld. A huge difference in purposes indeed. Or how a simple translation error can create a whole gambit of errors. i.e. Beelzebuth was originally Lord of the Flies. More recent evidence suggests that the translation was in error and he should have been identified as Lord of Lords.

Also, a good number of Demons were created from one Demon. I like to call this the "name game". A prime example of this is the Demon Asmodeous. He is also known as Asmoday, Amducious, and his name can be spelt a variety of ways. This is how one Demon becomes two. Ronove becomes Ronwe because of a simple spelling error handed on through the passage of time just as Astarte becomes Astaroth and Ashtaroth. Or Leviathan becomes Luithian and so on.

Because of this I have to say that studying different Demons and hierarchies can be a rewarding hobby and quite fascinating. In Demonolatry, the hierarchies different people use are usually based on personal preference. A lot of people use both Goetic Demons, and the Dukanté hierarchy, along with stand-alone Hebraic Demons who have no specific hierarchies. Generally the Goetia and Dukante hierarchies are the most popular.

Studying Demons can be a valuable to you as a practitioner of Demonolatry in that it can help you choose a Matron/Patron and will help you to know which Demons you wish to work with or honor for any variety of purposes. Please note that I like to point out that the definition of a Demon is not it's soul purpose. It's simply an aspect of that Demon. An option to give you a way to interpret it. We'll go into this in more depth next class.

Now I would like to discuss the nature of deity. Some people believe that deity is a single pure energy source while others believe in deity as a sentient being. This is a personal choice entirely. However, in Demonolatry a few basic rules apply to this - Every Demon has a counterpart, positive and negative polarity, male/female polarity, and every aspect in between. Let me point out that in saying male/female I am not talking physical, sexual gender as we know them. I am talking archetype polarity. Each gender represents a set of ideas or aspects that have been labeled in the feminine or masculine. You can see this polarity in the nine Demonic divinities as well as the aspects of each individual Demon. By saying a Demon is masculine or feminine, please note that I am not suggesting literal sex. Some people choose to see Leviathan as male while others see Leviathan as female. The same can be applied to Lucifer and many other Demons.

Let's use Belial as an example. Belial is the Earth elemental. His feminine aspect is mother, nurturer, and bountiful harvest. His masculine aspects are carnal nature, strength, stability, and balance. Each aspect can be helpful or hurtful depending on the perspective of the individual experience pertaining to that aspect.

One thing is for certain, whether energy or sentient entity - a deity is composed of matter. We worship (work with) this "matter". Through prayer we give it form and positive energy. In turn, it will likely return the favor. We'll discuss how prayer works a little more in the next lesson.

---

**Homework:** Read the chapter Introduction to Demonolatry.This will introduce you to the basic philosophies of Demonolatry. Also, go through the Demon directory and find a Demon who has several different spellings of his/her name. Note the variety.

## NOTES

# LESSON TWO

## Ritual Basics and Prayer

I am briefly going to go over the nine Demonic divinities. The first five are the five elements. They promote life and balance. They are the cycle of life and death, the year, etc. I know this sounds extremely Wiccan, but let me remind you that Demonolatry stems from pre-Christian religions, which were all very "Nature" oriented. The next divinities are Unsere - Life, and Eurynomous-Death. Polar opposite archetypes. Finally there is Healing and Destruction - Verrine and Amduscious. This is how the prayer cord is set up. Nine knots, nine divinities. If the prayer cord seems like a Catholic rosary to you, that's because the Catholics took the concept of the rosary from Demonolatry traditions.

**Ritual basics.** There are three basic purposes for ritual. 1. To honor or celebrate a Demon or set of ideas represented by that Demon. 2. For personal meditation, insight, and enlightenment. and 3. To focus on a specific purpose or goal (Magick). There are three parts to each ritual. 1. The Beginning - where you invite Demons into your ritual space. 2. The Middle - where the purpose of the ritual is recognized and acted on. 3. The End - where you thank each Demon for showing up politely before they "go home".

For each and every ritual - it is considered respectful to construct an elemental circle. In our tradition the circle promotes balance to ensure the proper flow of energy conducive to the type of atmosphere a Demon prefers. We build the circle out of respect for our wise friends and teachers. It is said that those people who take the time to construct a proper circle are considered worthy to gain wisdom and insight from the divine intelligences. This is a traditional practice.

Demonolators select a Matron/Patron Demon. They do this by matching the Demon's attributes to their own. Some people choose based on elemental signs and attributes, some people choose a Demon who resembles what they would like to be (alter-ego), some people choose a Demon who balances them out (i.e. a hot headed fire person may choose a stable, level headed earth Demon) and others choose a Demon based on a passion or hobby that greatly interests them. A good number of scholarly Demonolators have chosen Ronove (Ronwe) as their patron as he is the Demon who teaches languages and gives knowledge.

But - choosing a Matron/Patron does not mean you cannot work with other Demons. You can work with whichever Demons you choose. But it is an entirely different relationship than with a Matron/Patron. A lot of people have asked me about "Demon Guides." In Demonolatry the equivalent is a "Mentor or Teacher" Demon. This Demon picks you by presenting itself to you through a vision, supernatural experience, or one of the many forms of communication a Demon may use. You do not pick a mentor. That generally happens by default if you happen to strike the fancy of any particular Demon. It is very rare for a mentor to choose someone who has been practicing less than three years. However, there are exceptions to any rule. The Mentor/Teacher Demon gives spiritual lessons and enlightenment whereas the Matron/Patron is the "self" Demon. The "self" Demon helps you focus on and learn about you. It is an innate part of you. It can intensify your existing strengths and negate your weaknesses. This is why choosing the "proper" Matron/Patron is so important.

**A brief bit on prayer**: Prayer is the connection between you and deity. We do not pray to "get" stuff. Prayer is intention of will and the words spoken are the bridge to manifestation of that will. The divinities are there to promote the strength of will. See the Prayer chapter for more.

## HOMEWORK:

I like to suggest the following meditation (wherein you will not have to build an elemental circle - and you will be forgiven for it.). Go through the Demon dictionary or hierarchy section and find one Demon for your alter-ego, one Demon that is the complete opposite of your personality, find your elemental Demon, find one Demon that appeals to your aesthetic/image side, and find another Demon that deals with any strong hidden emotions you have. Make a list. Write down what appeals to you about each Demon. Note any patterns. Some of these Demons may be the same Demon. If you have a particular drawing to any one particular Demon - please note it.

Now I want you to build mental images for each Demon. For the next few nights, take a half hour to an hour and sit in a quiet room with a candle. Focus on one Demon from your list for each half hour session. Record your thoughts, feelings, tastes, smells, or sounds that you sensed during the meditation. Do this for each Demon. Once you have finished with each Demon - place all of your notes in front of you. Which Demon left the strongest impression on you? Keep doing this. It could take you weeks, months or years to complete this exercise. Once you've explored all the Demons that interest you, choose the ones you felt the strongest connections to. You will likely find yourself drawn to one in particular. The strongest one wherein you felt a "connection" is usually the BEST choice for a Patron/Matron

**Homework Part Two:** Construct an altar of offering. It can be outdoors or it can be inconspicuous. It can be the same altar you use for ritual. Upon this altar, make it a habit to leave offerings and prayers. Make journal entries describing your thoughts and feelings as well as results with this.

## NOTES

# LESSON THREE

## Personal Symbols of Power

**Sigils** and **Enns** are, essentially, focusing tools used to assist the practitioner with invoking a Demonic entity. They are considered to be the "calling cards" of a particular entity. Where do sigils come from? Some people believe the sigil is the spiritual "signature" of a Demonic entity. They are usually acquired through conversing with a particular spirit during an ascension meditation. Where do Enns come from? Enns are acquired through ascension as well. What is ascension? A deep meditative state wherein the priest(ess) or long-time adept communes with Demonic entities on a spiritual level. In absence of an Enn or sigil - you can create your own invitation in whatever language you feel comfortable with. You can also create a sigil for a Demon based on your perception of that Demon. There are many techniques for sigil creation. One is to use representative shapes, letters, or pictures. Or perhaps a design of your own creation that means something to you. Sigil magick is a course in and of itself. I suggest a book called *Practical Sigil Magic* by U.D. Frater and Ingird Fischer.

**Invocation vs. Evocation** - Demonolators invoke as opposed to evoke because evocation suggests conjuring an entity against its will. Invocation is more of a personal "invite", prayer, and allows the Demonic entity the right to its own free will. People who evoke Demons generally end up running back to Christianity after some scary experiences. Demons do not take kindly to attempted "forced" attendance.

**Hierarchies** used in Demonolatry include the Dukanté hierarchy and the Goetic hierarchy, which was discussed in the last lesson. We also briefly touched on the 9 Demonic divinities.

---

**Homework:** Continue with your meditation and prayer exercises. Make your own sigil using shapes you like, letters from your name, or pictorial representations of yourself. You can make this sigil a personal power source. Create an Enn for yourself to invoke your own courage and strength. Example - I am a predator, I am a seductress, I am strong! Keep these things private. They are personal to you. Whenever you feel weak or usurped of power, use your own sigil and Enn to take your power back.

## NOTES

# LESSON FOUR

## Courtesies/Sect Law and Celebration

Let's first discuss the Courtesies of the Sorcerer. Dukanté outlined the **Courtesies** as sect law to show the working harmony that should exist between all practitioners. The main concept underlying their [the Courtesies] design is that we are all a part of the whole and can learn and grow from one another even though our individual talents may vary. The Courtesies also warn against jealousy and power trips as ways of depleting our own personal power. You may want to print yourself a copy of the Courtesies and hang them someplace where you can review them daily.

Ideally, each practitioner of Demonolatry should hold the Courtesies as the highest form of sect law. Sect Law entails the codes of conduct by which each individual Demonolator should abide. It can vary from sect to sect. Some sect law (as the Courtesies) are all encompassing and universal. Others relate to group mechanics and human psychology. Breaking sect law hurts no one except the practitioner himself. **Sect Law** can be found in the section Proper Invocation, Tools, Ritual Execution and Layout

Holidays and Major Rites: The Demons most universally celebrated in Demonolatry are the seasonal changes represented by the elemental Demons, the standard spring initiation rite (First Rite to Leviathan) and the Rite to Eurynomous. While most Demons have their own individual days or months for celebration, the latter are the basics. Our calendar year is separated into four seasons - each being marked by either an equinox or solstice. Each part of the year makes up the whole. If you are familiar with many modern nature religions you will see that each

190

season represents a life cycle. This is true for Demonolatry as well. Our universe becomes balance and mathematical. Demonolatry is seeing everything from this viewpoint. The Religious holidays are extensions, expressions, and manifestations of these ideas. They are symbolic and balance and structure, as much as they are universal to our experience.

| Month/Day | Holiday |
|-----------|---------|
| March 21 | Equinox Rite to Lucifer |
| April 30 | Walpurgisnacht May Eve |
| June 22 | Solstice Rite to Flereous |
| September 21 | Equinox Rite to Leviathan |
| October 31 | All Hallows Eve Halloween |
| December 22 | Solstice Rite to Belial |

To learn more about each rite and its purpose or function within Demonolatry as a religion – see the Introduction to Demonolatry chapter.

The Major rites are a time for honoring the Demons, concentrating on individual parts of the whole, prayer, meditation, and celebration. These basic rites are primarily religious rites. Because Demonolatry in and of itself is a religion, this means that magick is not necessarily a part of the practice. Nonetheless, magick can be added to Demonolatry provided it is done in the construct of a ceremonial circle in worship of a particular Demon. Which, as mentioned in previous classes, is customary out of respect and tradition. We will go into magick next class period when we discuss the scientific and psychological principals of how and why magick works and why it compliments Demonolatry as a religion.

**Homework:** Continue with meditation and prayer exercises.

## NOTES

# LESSON FIVE

Obviously all of us knows by now that Demonolatry magick is largely ceremonial in that we take the time to build an atmosphere (circle) comfortable for the Demonic entities. We also take the time to build altars, shrines, and/or personal temples that create atmosphere for ourselves. These places and things are often laden with symbolism of our devotion to the Demons, our matrons and patrons, and so forth.

**The Ritual Tools -** Basic ritual tools include a bowl for burning things like incense and requests, candles, candle holders, a dagger (or knife of some sort), a chalice (or wine glass), pen & paper. Your ritual tools do not have to be elaborate. It can take years for you to acquire just the right tools. In the meantime, if you do not have the money or have not found what you want, you can certainly improvise using wine glasses for chalices, butter knives for daggers, sticks for swords, ashtrays to burn incense and requests in, and any type of candles you have. You may even elect to use no tools at all if that works for you.

However, over time, you will find that working magick is easier with the right tools. You will want at least two chalices, a cast iron burning bowl, an incense burner, candle holders that suit you, parchment, a ritual pen, ritual ink, a dagger, a sword, the sigil of your patron/matron painted or inscribed on an altar trivet (piece of wood), a large selection of candles (different colors). You should also acquire a basic set of ritual oleums, and incenses and build from there. Of course the easiest way is to make them yourself. In the beginning you can use store bought incense if all else fails. Use woody scents for earth (sandalwood, patchouli), light scents for air (bergamot), deep scents for fire (cinnamon or rose), and floral scents for water (lily).

For each individual ritual purpose, decide which element that purpose falls under, and use the appropriate scent.

Ritual tools should be used solely for ritual purposes. You can consecrate them by passing them through fire, scouring them with earth, rinsing them with water, and allowing them to air dry. Then you can do a rite wherein you "mentally" (or magickally) infuse each item with your will and the image of your patron/matron.

Remember, your tools are an extension of you. They are meant to help you focus and create atmosphere in your ritual space.

**The Altar** - For your altar, a piece of wood or a section of floor space will work just fine. For those of you who have more room - you can use an old desk or table as an altar. For others of you - a coffee table or the top of your entertainment center will work just as well. Always cover your altar with a cloth - to keep wax drippings off your furniture, carpet, and floors. Altar cloths are merely practical items. An old sheet will suffice. But if you are into ceremony, a nice piece of satin will do just as well.

**Ritual Space** - your ritual space should be quiet, warm, comfortable, and as free from distraction as it can be. It doesn't need to be a large space. Just enough space where you can walk around the altar and kneel in front of it. Some people choose to chalk or paint the outer boundary of their circle on the floor of the ritual space.

Outside the seemingly elaborate set up of tools, altars, et al, Demonic magick can seem quite basic. Most often the basic magical formula for Demonic magick includes oleums & incenses corresponding to the purpose of the magickal working, the writing of a request, the seal of the request in the magicians own blood, the burning of a request, and finally, a prayer or meditation time. Most magick is done during a rite in honor of a Demon that caters to the specific goal of the magick working. i.e. an Example might be that magick for love would be done during a rite to honor Rosier or any of the "Love & Friendship" Demons. In all other instances people choose to work magick during rites to their matron/patrons or to Satan.

All of this symbolism helps magick to function properly. *The most important point to remember is that Magick is not a quick fix for anything.*

Magick functions in several ways. First: It puts the magician's focus on a goal. Second: It directs appropriate energy toward that goal. Third: It motivates the magician to take action on that goal.

While some magick can and will work if you just sit back and wait for it to work - some of it will not work unless the magician takes post-rite action toward the goal. Example - if you do a rite to Belphegore and work magick during that rite to find a job - the job isn't going to just fall in your lap. You actually have to go out and fill out applications, go to interviews, and so on. Which brings me to the next point.

Let's break magick down into two types - psychological (self) magick wherein the magician takes an active role in creating positive energy and directing it toward a goal, and physical magick wherein the magician actually changes or creates the physical or existing state of something or someone.

In almost all instances, all magick is highly psychological. It attunes the magician's mind to the goal at hand, and preps the magician to reach that goal. It also lends favor to the magician via the energy put into the ritual. It most often requires post-ritual follow up.

Physical magick's purpose and direction are more clearly defined. This magick is actually more scientific. As psychological magick in and of itself can be seen as simply a ritual for "self-help" that motivates the individual doing it - scientific magick is actually something like esp or telekinesis where the magician's own will sends or directs matter (in the form of a pure energy) toward an object or person (including the self). Yes, I mean actually moving real molecules of energy after infusing them with purpose. Alone, this magick requires little to no follow up.

All magick is both psychological and physical to one degree or another. Breaking them up is just a way for the student to better understand how magick functions as a "whole".

Some people have a harder time with physical magick than others. Here are some common problems people with certain elemental makeups may have difficulty with:

- **Water** - when electricity hits water it becomes electric with no clear direction. People who have a lot of water in their natal charts may have a difficult time focusing.
- **Earth** - when electricity hits earth it grounds. People who have a lot of earth in their natal charts may have a difficult time building and sending energy before it grounds.

- **Air** - when electricity hits air it slices right through it. People who have a lot of air their natal charts may over extend their energies and either overdo things, or under do them to compensate. Air people should be very careful about directing negative energy as they can inadvertently hurt others or themselves by overdoing.
- **Fire** - when fire hits electricity it blends. People who have a lot of fire in their natal charts may expend all their energy building energy so that they have none left to direct that energy. They may end up feeling exhausted after ritual work.

So where do Demons come in? Calling on Demons whose correspondences match the magickal working benefits the magician and the Demon. It benefits the magician in that it draws additional pure energy so the magician is not over-exerting himself in creating it all himself (which makes the magick much more effective), and it also helps the magician gain clearer focus and insight into the purpose of the magick - which ultimately helps with easier direction. Plus, Demons will help to "send" or direct that energy in conjunction with the magician making the magick work faster. By doing the magickal working inside a structured rite - the magician feeds the Demon positive energy through prayer, devotion, and energy built during the rite. A happy Demon is a helpful Demon!

Not to mention that true Demonic magick involves worshiping and respecting the Demon, which in turn elicits respect and help from the Demon. This is why Demonic magick coupled with Demonolatry works so much better than many of the other forms of folk and ceremonial magick - because both the Demon and practitioner benefit positively from the rite. Balance is maintained because as much energy is given as is taken.

**Homework:** Figure out your elemental breakdown based on your natal chart (each sign has an element and we each have 12 signs in our charts – see elemental balancing for more information) and correct any noted imbalances using the elemental balancing ritual.

## NOTES

# Meditation & Ascension

This section contains the meditation lessons and information about ascension. Students are asked to work the meditations in order.

The first section is the Basic Meditation Core meant to teach the student how to meditate and to help him build a regular meditation practice. This core is also accompanied by a set of four readings that will teach the student about meditation and suggest further study and reading.

The second set of lessons make up the Demonolatry Meditation Core. There are no readings, but the work is far more extensive.

**A note for teachers:** These lessons ask the student to record their meditations. You might have them verbally share their meditation experiences with you or you might ask to see their journal entries. The time frame set for study is one week per exercise or meditation. The same goes for readings. One reading per week. Encourage students to not rush any faster than this or they might miss the full benefits of the meditation core.

**A note about Ascension:** It is advisable that pre-initiates and initiates refrain from attempting ascension practice until they have developed a regular meditation practice. This means, in the very least, that the student should be able to meditate up to a minimum of one half hour.

## Health Warning

Persons who are experiencing emotional discord or depression should not practice meditation, ascension, or channeling. Dream work and other astral work is also not advised. Meditative states are known to increase depression and emotional discord. The author and publisher are not responsible for any person who might choose to ignore this important information.

# BASIC MEDITATION CORE

## Recording your meditations

After each meditation you should record your experience in the following manner:

Date
Meditation Description and Duration:
How I felt before the meditation.
How I felt during the mediation.
How I felt immediately afterward.
What kept popping into my mind during the meditation?
Smells I noticed:
Sounds I noticed:
Physical sensations:
Emotional sensations:
Thoughts or Comments:

If you cannot fill in all of the spaces right away - don't force it. Allow yourself time to reflect on the experience and then go back and fill in the blanks at a later time. Noting how you felt is especially important. Did you feel cramping in your legs? Were you aware of certain muscles tensing up? These could be meditation posture problems, which could be indicative that you need to find a different sitting position.

**PLEASE NOTE**
If you have been diagnosed with clinical depression or bipolar disorder DO NOT meditate if you are experiencing a severe onset of depression or if you are feeling suicidal. Studies indicate that some people who meditate during depression can become even more depressed.

# READING ONE

## WHY MEDITATE?

For the Demonolator meditation has many benefits. First, it helps to develop focusing skills. This inevitably will help you with focusing your will during magickal workings. Second, it helps to open your mind to more easily connect with Demonic entities. Lastly, meditation will, over time, fine-tune your focusing and awareness leading to a more effective ascension practice. People who jump into ascension without strong meditation skills often find it difficult to practice ascension because they have not yet developed the stillness of mind and focus needed to attain that state of awareness that can allow the mind access to the Demonic plane. It can also help us to tap into our natural abilities for divination and internal wisdom.

On a more basic level, meditation can teach us how to control how we respond to stress triggers, teach us to observe our emotions/thoughts/reactions, and can lead to an overall heightened state of awareness, relaxation, and well-being.

## HOW TO MEDITATE:

"How" does a person learn to meditate? Many people I've met seem overly concerned about technique as if learning to meditate is something akin to learning how to play the flute. As someone who has been meditating for almost 20 years, I'm here to tell you that it's not that complex.

First, learning "how" to meditate is not as hard as people

seem to think. You merely sit in a comfortable spot in a comfortable position and focus your attention on something, whether it is an object, idea, or your own breath.

What *is* difficult is learning how to focus your attention on something for long durations of time. There is no tried and true technique for how to do this. It cannot be "taught" so to speak. Either you have focus or you don't. Most of us need to "develop" our attention spans (focus) to help us learn to meditate for longer durations. This means we start out meditating for short durations and gradually learn patience and ways of keeping ourselves focused as we go. Learning to meditate is really a hands-on thing. You can't read a book or have someone tell you how to do something, and then expect to just "know" how it's done, then have 100% excellent results from then on out.

Meditation is, for all intents and purposes, the calming of the mind and directing focus. This leads to revelation, insight, and relaxation. So no matter how you meditate or how long you do it, you really can't do it "wrong", and you can't hurt yourself (unless you are depressed - see class introduction for the warning). There is no one definitive way to meditate and what works for one person will not always work for the next.

Comfort is an important part of any meditation practice because discomfort can become a distraction. Wear loose, comfortable clothing and make sure your quiet space is at a comfortable temperature and free from distractions.

**There are two more things that may help enhance your meditation practice.**

1. **Posture.** The way you sit is very important. There are many positions you can try. The key point is you should be comfortable without being so comfortable that you fall asleep (unless you are using a specific meditative technique to cure insomnia or need to put yourself in the proper state-of-mind for various dream workings). Allow your hands to fall comfortable on your knees palms down, or you can rest the back of your hands on your knees, all fingers bent slightly upward, with your thumb and index finger touching. Additionally you can hold your hands to your chest and with your fingers create a triangle over the heart chakra.

*Here are several of the positions you can try:*

-Sit in a chair with your feet firmly on the ground.
-Sit cross-legged.
-Sit in half-lotus.
-Sit in full lotus.
-Sit against a wall with your legs stretched out in front of you.
-Use a meditation cushion to lift your hips, properly align the spine, and lower your legs to the floor. The meditation cushion provides extra support.

If you are unfamiliar with Lotus pose (a preferred sitting position for many), look it up on the internet. There are many sites with information on lotus pose.

Correct body alignment is important. Your head should sit squarely on top of your shoulders and your spine should remain supple. Your sitting bones should firmly have contact with the ground (if not using a meditation cushion). Whether or not this is comfortable for you is another story. Whatever you do, don't slouch and try not to tense up your muscles (back, shoulders, or neck) nor should you straighten your back too much because it will eventually tense up. Every part of you should be relaxed, including your forehead, tongue, and throat.

2. **Concentration.** Most people will find that they have a shorter attention span than they imagined. Your first meditations may only last 5-10 minutes, but will gradually increase as you begin to feel more comfortable meditating. For meditations about "nothing" specifically, many people find it difficult to concentrate on nothing. This is completely normal. Easier meditations are generally guided, or allow the mind some subject matter to chew on. Start with something to concentrate on. Move on to "nothing" later on.

### *Some tips for maintaining focus:*

-Always start by becoming aware of your breath. Take long, even breaths. Relax. Then switch your focus to the subject matter. Allow your thoughts to pass through your mind without judging them or reacting. Become an observer.


-Use physical objects to focus on, then close your eyes. Candle flames, pictures, statues, or sigils may help you stay focused. When you start to lose focus open your eyes, then will yourself back to the here and now. Additionally you may choose to allow your mind to wander. There is no right or wrong way. Sometimes allowing the mind to wander will reveal something about the original subject matter. If you feel the need to focus try to speak aloud to yourself, or recite a mantra to get back on track. Whatever works.

# EXERCISE 1

## MEDITATION AND THE BREATH

In Eastern philosophy, the breath is the spirit. It is the bridge between the body and mind. Most of us don't breathe right. We take quick, shallow breaths with intermittent deep breaths. People who smoke will almost always have this problem. People who are stressed out tend to hold their breath. As a result of improper breathing you might find yourself sighing or yawning a lot. You may find you're exhausted half way through your day. All of this is a result of not getting enough oxygen. For the magician low energy reserves and exhaustion (i.e. not enough oxygen) can adversely effect how effective your magical workings are. Part of a meditation practice can be about learning how to control your breath.

*What kind of breather are you? Become aware of to how you breathe.*

## BREATH EXERCISES

1. Sit comfortable and inhale and exhale completely. Once you have exhaled all the air from your lungs, sharply contract your abdomen and force the expulsion of air from your nose and breathe in just as quickly through the nose. Do this 20 times. Focus on steady, quick breaths that focus on the expulsion of air. Work your way up to three sets of 20, breathing normally in between sets.

2. Lye on your back with arms to your sides. Exhale completely then draw a slow, deep breath in through your nose, expanding your abdomen and lungs. Contract your throat slightly and make a soft hissing sound as you exhale and empty your lungs completely.

3. Sit comfortably and exhale with a sigh. This will reset your diaphragm. Breathe in through your nose to the slow count of 7. Hold your breath for a moment. Then exhale through your nose for a count of 7 and again hold your breath for a moment. Do this several times.

4. Sit comfortably and place the middle finger of your right hand on your forehead (third eye chakra). Rest your thumb on your right nostril and rest your ring and pinky on your left nostril. Inhale and exhale then close your right nostril with your thumb. Inhale through the left nostril to the count of five. Close both nostrils and hold your breath to the count of five. Lift your thumb and exhale through your right nostril to the count of 5. Repeat on the other side.

# READING TWO

## THE DIFFERENT TYPES OF MEDITATION

**Guided:** A guided meditation is when another person leads your imagination on a journey. In this instance, the person meditating simply focuses on the voice of the guide and allows her mind to follow. You simply observe your mind's reaction as if watching a movie. There are numerous tapes and CD's of guided meditations available. Or you can record your own.

**Relaxation:** For stress reduction, relaxation meditation is popular. Generally, for a relaxing meditation, you focus on your breath. Breathe deeply and evenly, and systematically start at your feet and tighten and release muscle groups from your feet to your head so that you are relaxed. This type of meditation can be done lying down, but you may fall asleep before finishing. It's a great meditation to try if you have trouble sleeping, or you have a lot of tension. The point of relaxation meditation is to quiet the mind. Try focusing on the silence – it works wonders, especially in the modern world where we are constantly bombarded with external stimuli.

**Insight:** This type of meditation (sometimes called concentrative meditation) is used for soul searching and discovering your own innate wisdom. It can also be used to develop a deeper connection to your spiritual Self. You start off focusing on the breath. Deep, relaxed breathing will help bring you to an aware meditative state, then you shift your focus onto the subject matter of the meditation, and allow your mind to freely explore the subject in its own way. Staying focused on the subject becomes most of the battle. Some people have said insightful meditation is something akin to relaxed daydreaming. In a sense, it is. Your relaxed, aware state allows the mind to make correlations, and reveal insight more easily than everyday consciousness. Many people will use insight meditation as a means of solving bothersome worries and emotional, or life problems.

Overall, meditation, like anything, is something you learn over time.

Breathing exercises, gentle yoga sessions beforehand, and listening to guided meditations may help you on your journey. Experiment and explore. Eventually you will find a meditation technique right for you.

# EXERCISE 2

## BRIEF MEDITATION 1

Sit with your spine comfortably erect. Take a deep breath and exhale completely. Inhale through your nostrils imagining a standing wave rising through your body and up your spine. Exhale through the nostrils and imagine a warm light emanating from every pore in your skin. Do this for five minutes.

# READING THREE

## MAKING MEDITATION A REGULAR PRACTICE

It can be difficult, with a busy lifestyle, to find time to meditate. If you find you are having this difficulty, you may want to try meditating before bed, right when you wake up, or when the baby is taking a nap (for you parents). For those of you with more time and more stamina, you may choose to meditate longer or more frequently. Just like anything, making meditation a habit can be difficult, as it requires you to make modifications to your existing daily routine. It's easier to make lifestyle modifications if you start out slowly and gradually increase the time you meditate from week to week or month to month.

Start out by meditating twice a week for fifteen minutes each. Keeping a regular schedule for your meditation practice will make it easier for you to stick with it. Choose two days of the week and a specific time for your practice. Once you are in your meditation space, set a timer or alarm clock. Make sure your meditation space is quiet, free from distraction, and at a comfortable temperature.

## MEDITATION AND YOGA

Aleister Crowley was big on yoga for a reason. Yoga is about calming the mind, becoming aware of the Self, focusing, having discipline over the body, and increasing oxygen flow to the blood. All of this can greatly enhance your ritual work. You might consider taking on a light yoga practice session before meditation to get your body and mind warmed up for extended meditation. I suggest Yoga Journal's Yoga for Meditation with Rodney Yee. You can probably find it at your local health or fitness store as well as online. The tapes cost around $15 each.

# EXERCISE 3

## BREIF MEDITATION 2

This is a modified version of one of the meditations in the next section. This meditation comes from the book: *Qabbalistic Concepts - Living the Tree* by William Gray.

Sit in a darkened room (the darker the better) and relax. Become aware of your breath. Take deep, even breaths. Relax. Focus your attention to your third eye. Think of nothingness. Hear the silence. Focus on that while imagining the blackness as the whole. Imagine yourself as a tiny speck in the blackness. The blackness is nothingness. Nil. Yet it is all encompassing. It is everything and nothing. Allow yourself to become one with the blackness. You become the blackness. You are the whole. You are everything, and nothing. Remain aware of your breath. Do this for 10 minutes.

# READING FOUR

**Helpful Books/Kits:**

***Insight Meditation: A Step by Step Course on How To Meditate*** – Salzburg & Goldstein, This is a complete course on insight meditation. While it is guided by Buddhist philosophy, I highly recommend it because the basics are there. The kit will cost approximately $30. You can probably find it at your local bookstore or metaphysical shop. You can just buy the workbook in paperback for about $15 bucks. The kit comes with the workbook, two guided meditation CDs and study cards.

**Online Resources**: Since online pages can disappear, I've tried to include links that seem stable. However, if you notice a link not working, please feel free to e-mail my publisher at ofs.admin@gmail.com

**Using meditation to learn to relax:**
http://www.learningmeditation.com/relax.htm

**Using meditation to help with health issues:**
http://1stholistic.com/Meditation/hol_meditation.htm - This is a wonderful site (scroll down past the ads) that details the health benefits of meditation.

http://www.newscientist.com/article.ns?id=dn8317 - Results of a meditation study and its effects on health and performance.

**Online Meditations:**
http://www.learningmeditation.com/room.htm - You need Real Player to listen to these guided meditations geared toward relaxation and awareness.

http://www.dailyzen.com/ - An online zen meditation resource.

http://www.insightmeditation.org/meditation.htm - An online Dharma meditation resource.

http://www.666blacksun.com/Power_Meditations.html - Joy of Satan meditations. I may not agree with their theology, but some of their meditations are good and can be modified to your specific wants and needs.

# EXERCISE 4

*This is also a modified meditation from the next Core lesson. In the original meditation it is meant to heighten the bond between the individual and their Matron/Patron. In this instance the meditation is meant as a means for you to explore the various energies of different Demons.*

Meditate on a Demon of your choice using its sigil as a focal point. As your eyes begin to feel heavy, feel the Demon's energy surrounding you. See a soft light emanating from your skin. Allow the Demon's energy to come in contact with that light. Surrender to the Demon's energy and let it flow through you. Remember your breath. Relax. Allow all emotions, feelings, and thoughts to flow freely. Do this for as long as you feel comfortable. Make note of how long you spent in meditation.

***Note - the point of this exercise is not to BECOME the Demon. That is impossible. However, you can merge with a Demon by intertwining energies empathically.***

# Demonolatry
# Meditation Core

## MEDITATION 1

The first lesson is about being a part of the whole. Each of us is merely a speck in the vast universe. Yet, each of us is a needed part of the whole. Without your essence, the whole would only be a fraction of itself. We are all composed of the matter of the whole of the universe. Matter cannot be created or destroyed - it can only change form regardless if its composition is sentient or not.

This modified meditation comes from the book: Qabbalistic Concepts - Living the Tree by William Gray. I highly recommend this book as a part of your study as it is extremely interesting, and some of it very applicable to Demonolatry.

Sit in a darkened room (the darker the better) and relax. Become aware of your breath. Take deep, even breaths. Relax. Focus your attention to your third eye. Think of nothingness. Imagine the blackness as the whole. Imagine yourself as a tiny speck in the blackness. The blackness is nothingness. Nil. Yet it is all encompassing. It is everything and nothing. Allow yourself to become one with the blackness. You become the blackness. You are the whole. You are everything, and nothing. Remember to keep breathing.

## MEDITATION 2

(M/P)atron's are the spiritual extension of the self. They are a part of you, your alter ego, a balance in something you lack, or an extension of what you would like to become. They are ever present within you and become stronger after your dedication. Connecting with them through meditation brings realization, wisdom, and a deeper understanding of the self.

This meditation is as follows: Meditate on your M/Patron. Allow their energy to surround you. Surrender to it. Merge with it. Remember your breath. Relax. Allow all emotions, feelings, thoughts to flow freely. Their thoughts become your thoughts and vice versa. You are intertwined with your M/Patron. [Note - the point of this exercise is not to BECOME the Demon. That is impossible. However, you can merge with a Demon by intertwining energies empathically.]

## MEDITATION 3

Just as you meditated on your M/Patron - you can meditate on any Demon, symbol, picture, or person. If it helps your focus to have a physical representation to concentrate on - take it with you to your meditation space. Sometimes, meditating on a specific deity, item, or symbol makes its meaning clearer to us. Example - I could never get the hang of reading rune stones. Finally, I sat down and decided that once a night for however long it took, I would sit down with one stone at a time and meditate on it, then write down what it meant to me. As a result, I ended up with a rune dictionary of my own design.

Now, when I do rune readings, they are almost 95% accurate every time. This example is meant to show that sometimes meditations allows things to unravel right before your eyes because you stopped to take notice of how these things make *you* feel and what you sense from them empathically. Allowing your natural empathy to take over is a spiritual process that deepens our sense of individuality and wholeness. To learn more about a specific Demon whose origins seem a mystery to you, all you need to do is sit down and meditate on her for a time. Gently, she will *reveal* herself to you by how you spiritually relate to her.

Choose a Demon, symbol, or tarot card and meditate on it. Be sure to note your usual meditation notes as well as what the Demon, symbol, or tarot card revealed to you. What was its appeal to you in the first place? Did it lose its appeal after you meditated on it? Did it become more appealing? Explore why, and how.

# MEDITATION 4

## Solving External Problems through Demonolatry.

The best way for me to present our next topic is to tell a story. A few years ago, a young man was having difficulties in his relationships with women. It seemed that just when he thought a relationship was going somewhere he found something unappealing about the woman, or she would find something unappealing about him and the relationship would immediately end. As a result, he was very lonely and tired of the dating scene. Being a Demonolator, he did numerous rites to Rosier and Astarte. While they worked, their results were short lived. Finally, his good friend and high priest suggested he write all of his relationship problems out in a journal, then pick one problem at a time, then meditate to Rosier while simultaneously thinking about the problem. In doing this - the young man discovered he had fears of commitment and had the habit of choosing women who were also afraid of commitment. By facing his fear of commitment, he was able to finally move past the difficulty and into a long-term relationship - curing his loneliness.

The point of this story is that we must realize sometimes ritual and prayer are only temporary help. The solutions to our problems are within ourselves. Everything is interconnected. Demons can only help you once you've decided to help yourself by examining the self. Almost all external problems (outside death and taxes and things beyond your control like natural disasters) are "self" related.

External Problems might include: relationships, money issues, work issues and so on.

Make a list of all your "external" problems including finances, job, family, stress, and so forth. Choose what you consider to be your biggest problem. Meditate to a corresponding Demon. What are your results? Systematically go through each problem like this. It could take days, it could take months. Once you feel you have examined each problem, do a rite in which you burn a piece of paper with those problems written on it.

## MEDITATION 5

Now we will examine internal problems much like we examined the external ones. Internal problems include fear, anger, anxiety, stress, body image, health, and negative emotions. All of these things cause us fatigue, unhappiness, and impede on our general well being. What many people fail to realize is that the mind has the power to heal us physically, spiritually, and emotionally just as it has the power to cause us problems of the same nature. To be spiritually content requires that we are happy/comfortable with ourselves and our lives. It requires that we take full responsibility for ourselves. A good example of this is when someone says something to hurt your feelings, you choose to let it bother you. One way of negating this negative feeling is by telling the other person that they have hurt your feelings. This is what it means to take responsibility for your emotions, actions, re-actions, and so forth.

Make a list of all your "internal" problems. Choose what you consider to be your biggest problem. Meditate to a corresponding Demon. What are your results? Systematically go through each problem like this. It could take days, it could take months. Once you feel you have examined each problem, do a rite in which you burn a piece of paper with those problems written on it.

## MEDITATION 6

Now that you have concentrated on your "problems" - we are going to focus on your strengths. We all need a spiritual ego boost now and again. We all go through low times where we feel bad about ourselves, depressed, or feel like our lives are terrible. It's necessary for us to have the low times as well as the high times so that we can fully experience what it is to be human and to explore ourselves more deeply. You will always have lows and highs no matter how much self-work you do. However, the more self- work you do, it is more likely the fewer life problems you will have.

This meditation is a big one, and like the past two, it is a life long journey.

You are going to make three lists on separate pieces of paper/pages in your journal.

1. **Make a list of all your weaknesses**. Be objective, not self-destructive. Example - don't say - I'm a lazy, fat ass. Say - I have a lack of motivation. Find a Demon who is opposite your weakness or who you feel would not have that weakness. Example - one of my weaknesses is that I worry too much what other people think of me. I chose Lucifer to negate this weakness because, to me, Lucifer is enlightened and has an ego. He doesn't care what people think of him. When you are done with your meditation - write down things you can do to negate the weakness. Allow the Demon to reveal insight into the situation. Go with your gut feelings because that is her advice to you.

2. **Now make a list of all your strengths** - good things people have said about you, things you really like about yourself (now is NOT the time to be humble!), things you

do really well, ways you have or can help others, things that make you feel good and so on. List only POSITIVE things.

3. **Finally, make a list of your goals** - all the things you want to do in your life. My goal list includes: "Have a large castle in the mountains somewhere!" Make your goals grand and lofty. Make some of them realistic like: "Get the house cleaned before Saturday afternoon at 2pm." Now go through and mark each goal in one of three ways - short term (1 day to 6 months), long term (6 months to five years), future (after five years). You'll probably find the loftier the goal - the less important it really is. Don't be afraid to have long term or future goals. When I was 17 and decided I wanted to be a writer I said aloud in a room full of people: "By the time I'm 30 - I will have my own column." When I was 27, I got my own computer column in a national trade magazine. So you see - no long-term goal is impossible or unrealistic. Perhaps some day you will drive a Jaguar or own a home in Beverly Hills. Who knows. The clearer your focus, the easier it is to make your dreams and goals your reality.

**Once a week** - take a strength that relates to one short- term goal and find a corresponding Demon. Meditate on the situation. Do a rite to focus on the situation. Include prayers for insight during your meditations. Complete the goal. As you meet each goal - cross it off your list. Refresh your goal and strength list as you discover new things about yourself and what you want from your life. I revise mine twice a year.

**Once a month** - take one strength that compliments one long-term goal and find a corresponding Demon. Meditate on the situation. Do a rite to focus on the

221

situation. Include prayers for insight in your daily prayers. Eventually you WILL complete the goal.

Never try to conquer a big goal too quickly. Take small baby steps and eventually you will get what you want. Many actors and actresses have to go through tons of auditions before they become famous. Many a writer was rejected hundreds of times before being published for the first time. Many princesses had to go through a slew of frogs to find a prince. You may have to take lower paying jobs for a few years before you land your dream job. The point is: *Anything worth having or doing takes time.*

# Ascension

Ascension is a state of ascended consciousness reached through deep meditation. It allows the practitioner to commune with Demons on the Demonic plane and helps you to speak to the higher Self.

Do not practice ascension if you have not developed a strong meditation practice because it can drain your energy in such a way that you can fall ill, experience dizziness or nausea, and it can even cause depression.

The following rituals should be used without modification until you feel comfortable in your own ability to modify them for your needs.

# To Ascend to the Demonic Plane
*Richard Dukanté*

1 part rose
2 parts chamomile
1 part camphor

Mix into oil and anoint temples. Place a parchment on which is drawn 12 Demonic sigils of your discretion. Place this beneath your mattress or beneath your sleeping place. Light a white candle. Place an image of yourself outside yourself and project your consciousness into it. Go through black caverns and face your fears one by one. Only then shall you emerge onto the plane. If you do not, your fears have not been faced.

# Invocation To Speak With a Demon
*(from Dukanté grimoire)*

The Demon Conjuration Of Richard Dukanté (circa 1963 - the Grimoire of Richard Dukante Book 1 Page 50) Being a working wherein the Demon of the practitioner's choice may be called upon willfully.

Upon the alter must stand three tapers. One of Black, One of White, One of the castor's element. Within the Castor's taper the Demon's name must be inscribed upon it along with the name of Satan. [meaning actual - SATAN]

Present also must be the dagger and chalice of water taken from a flowing river or from the falling rain.

The invocation incense shall be burned within the thurible during the entire rite: 2 Parts Sandalwood, 5 Parts Graveyard Dust [mullein], and 3 Parts Devil's Claw.

You Shall begin by lighting the tapers upon the alter after having writ the aforementioned inscriptions on the center taper. Set the incense alight within the thurible. Cast the circle by invoking each element in the language of Demons                                                                -

- Earth - Belial - Lirach Tasa Vefa Wehlic Belial

**Translation - Earth protect this Soil , Lord Belial**

- Air - Lucifer - Renich Tasa Uberaca Biasa Icar Lucifer

**Translation - Air protect the surrounding sky, Lord Lucifer**

- Fire - Flereous - Ganic Tasa Fubin Flereous

**Translation - Fire protect the flame, Lord Flereous**

- Water - Leviathan- Jedan Tasa Hoet Naca Leviathan

**Translation - Water protect our circle, Lord Leviathan.**

Begin the Invocation: *I, [your name], do invite thee, [Demon's name]. In the name of Satan, I request you come forth.*

Hence you shall draw your own blood from your palm and let three drops fall into the chalice. Mingle it with the water and invite all present to drink from it. Do not drink from your own blood lest you invite the Demon into you.

You shall draw a circle upon the ground the width of the taper at least. Within this circle, inscribe the sigil of the Demon you doth conjure. If this sigil is unavailable, use an inverse pentagram or DZ. You shall pour the remainder of the chalice contents within the circle - for it is your energy the Demon will use to rise. " 'Tis this energy that is blood."

Over the circle you must say:

***Reayha bacana lyan remé quim [name of Demon].***

Place the castor's candle within the circle. From this circle - the Demon shall emerge from the flame and you may speak with him freely until the candle is extinguished.

# Channeling Demons

Demons can be channeled by willfully allowing them into your body. The purpose for this practice is to allow a Demon to speak through the person channeling. There is no reason to practice channeling unless you are in a group setting and seeking Demonic wisdom. Also, not everyone can channel Demons because not all of us are good conduits. The type of person who is most apt to have success is the one who has some medium ability, and who can open him or her self up to the experience willfully.

The procedure for channeling is similar to an ascension. You must go into a meditative state, make contact, merge energy with the Demon, and then invite the Demon into you. The meditation exercises in this book including merging exercises can help. Channeling should only be attempted if you have developed a regular meditation practice, are not depressed, and do not have any emotional turmoil in your life. Oftentimes, it is suggested that young persons aged 12-20 be careful when practicing ascension or channeling because hormonal imbalances can intensify the raw energy and cause deep emotional discord. So do take heed these warnings.

When a Demon comes through a person the sensation is very strange. It is like having a higher consciousness inside you and seeing through two sets of eyes at the same time. While it may be difficult to explain, be assured the Demon will leave when asked. If you are polite to Demons, then they will treat you with that same respect. It never fails that those who treat Demons with disrespect will be treated disrespectfully in kind. This is why some people have negative experience after negative experience with Demons. They've done something disrespectful like commanding, threatening, or they have a deep- rooted fear of the Demonic.

## Exercises for Building Energy and Grounding

The following exercises can be practiced to amplify energy or to replenish used energy. One can also be used to ground excess energy. Also see the modified pillar ritual later in this book for replenishing depleted energy. These exercises have been practiced since the time of the ancient Egyptians and variations can be found in many schools of modern occult and new age thought.

## EXERCISE 1

First, sit in front of the altar. Put your palms together and rub vigorously to increase the blood flow. Your hands will feel hot. At that point, pull your palms apart three inches and you will start to feel the energy build between your palms. You'll actually feel resistance (try to put your palms together again - you'll feel the resistance) once the energy has built up enough. Then you can direct that energy for elemental balancing, magickal work, or you can bring it into yourself as necessary. You can also give it as an offering to a Daemon if you so choose. Use this technique with the Elemental Balancing ritual included in the "Positive Workings" section of this book.

**Experiment:** Another thing you might attempt is to do this in a darkened room or at night, across from a metal object or a chain link fence. Once you feel you have built enough energy, hurl it at the metal object and you might see sparks. Very few people are able to do this. I can't either. In the last 18 years I've met one person with this ability.

## EXERCISE 2

Sit cross-legged or in lotus pose in front of your altar. Put your arms at your sides. Place your left hand palm down and your right hand palm up. Now imagine a circle of energy surrounding you and moving clockwise around you. You will begin to feel the energy moving through one hand, around, and through the other. Do this then try Exercise One immediately afterward and see how you feel.

**EXERCISE 3**

The next time you feel anxiety, stress, agitation, or anger do the following: Sit on the ground and place both hands, palms down, firmly on the ground. Take three deep, measured breaths. Allow the solidity of the ground to rise through you to every point of your body, then sink back down through your hands into the ground. This will ground you. Try it outside in the grass, or on the dirt. Note the differences of natural ground to carpet, tile, or wood flooring.

## Energy Vibrations

One of the things you should know about energy is that each thing, inanimate or not, created by us or not, has a certain vibration all its own. The molecules of each thing vibrate at a certain frequency. If you understand string theory, you may better understand this. This means that each emotion causes your energy to vibrate differently than it's normal level. These vibrations can attach themselves to inanimate things. Instinctively, humans are in tune with this. But with our modern world of constant stimuli, we have learned to ignore the vibrations of everything that surrounds us. The next exercise is meant for you to feel and attune yourself with the various vibrations of numerous objects and emotions. In turn, you will learn how to attune yourself to Demonic energy, your own energies, and the energy created during ritual. The first is a great exercise to do in a group setting (even if those in the group do not share your beliefs).

## PART ONE

Have members of the group each bring an object belonging to someone else. They should not tell anyone who the object belongs to, but they should know something about the person it belonged to. In this exercise each person goes into a room by themselves where the objects have been placed and one by one, each person feels each object and writes down the impressions he or she gets from it.

Once everyone has participated, the objects are retrieved from the person who brought it and everyone convenes in one room. Then, each person shares what he or she thought of each object. The person who brought the object then shares who the item belonged to and what that person was like. You'll be amazed at what some people were able to pick up about an object just by feeling it's vibrational energy.

## PART TWO

Go around your house and feel the vibrations of the various items around your home. Feel something new, feel something old, feel something you love, and feel something you don't really care for. Note the differences in the vibrations of each object.

## PART THREE

The next time you are in ritual, feel the vibrations of all your ritual tools and note the vibrations you felt during the ritual. Begin doing this regularly. This is important because once you learn to distinguish from a positive or negative vibration, the better you'll be able to determine when your ritual tools are due for balancing and cleansing.

# Astral Projection

Astral projection is the act of separating the astral body (spirit or consciousness) from the physical body and its journey into the universe. It differs from an out-of-body experience (or near death) in that Astral Projection happens voluntarily. There are three types of astral projection. Mental projection, as in meditation where you take your mind from your body, astral projection, where both the astral body and mind leave the physical body, and etheric projection where the astral body, mind, and spirit all leave the body.

A common method of achieving astral projection is to go into a meditative state and feel each your breath and energy centering on all of your charkas. Then, from the third eye chakra (sometimes also the heart chakra), you willfully rise from your body.

Then, the astral self can travel freely into the universe or the world as wanted.

See the chart on the next page for information where the chakras fall.

# CHAKRA CHART

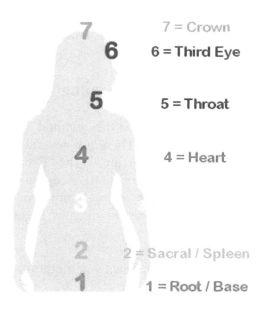

7 = Crown

6 = Third Eye

5 = Throat

4 = Heart

2 = Sacral / Spleen

1 = Root / Base

## Astral Temples

For some people a physical temple is impossibile. This may be the case for the practitioner who lives with others who are not Demonolators. In this case, the practitioner may choose to build an astral temple. An astral temple is a place in the mind where you can privately practice ritual, meditation, and prayer. Your temple can be as big or small as you want, and can be equipped with any tools you envision. There, you can freely meet and talk with Demons and other people with whom you've made prior arrangements to meet there. You can travel to the temple astrally or through mental projection.

To start, do a meditation in which you envision your perfect temple. Go through and place the details in this place. See it in color. Walk around it to get a feel for your space. The more often you visit your temple, the clearer and solid it will become.

## Lucid Dreaming

Lucid Dreaming is another method of communing with the Demonic Divine. There are several methods you can use to cause lucid dreams. The first is to do a meditation just before you go to sleep where you are meeting someone at your astral temple, or where you invoke a Demon to be present in your dream to impart wisdom.

Some additional methods you might try include:

- Place a sigil of the Demon you wish to commune with under your mattress or pillow.
- Burn an incense that promotes lucid dreaming.
- Invoke an elemental circle around your bed.

You may also choose to employ all of the above methods at the same time depending on how much focus of will necessary to help you achieve a lucid dreaming state. The more experienced you become, the less preparation or outside help you'll need. Much like learning ascension, you can learn to will yourself to astral project, go to the astral temple, or have lucid dreams.

There are plenty of books out there that go into the astral and dream worlds more thoroughly. So we'll leave this topic now and move onward.

# Holy Day Rites & Rites of Nine

### Basic Rite To Belial

The Altar must face the North most point of the ritual chamber. A candle is set at each elemental point. The elemental Demons are invoked by use of the enns with the dagger. Invoke Lucifer first and work clockwise, leaving Belial for last. An incense of patchouli and mullein invokes atmosphere.

Light the candles from Lucifer to Belial. Then - Carrying a bowl of sand in one hand and a dagger in the other (doesn't matter which) approach each point and kneel reciting the enn for Belial and dip the dagger into the sand and sprinkle it at each point. (If you have carpet in your ritual chamber, place a bowl at each point and let the sand fall into each bowl) Finally, invite the fifth element from the center of the ritual space.

Kneel at the altar in prayer: "We pray thee Belial, bestow upon us the strength of your design. Give us the gift of stability or to start the New Year free of past stalemates. Allow our thoughts and actions to be our protection. Be present that we shall not falter in our decisions. We are as the stable earth. We humbly pay homage to thee in our offer of earth that you may know our respect for your vast strength. We offer requests of new beginnings, strength, and mundane matters that we may employ your creation to do so. Hail Belial. Lord and Master of Earth."

Then comes the typical ritual body in which requests of new beginnings, strength, and mundane matters are burned within the altar or primary ritual space fire. (i.e. a bowl, incense burner, or bonfire.) Use the remaining sand to smother the fire once the requests have been burnt. The ashes must be crushed to a fine powder and later buried. Some sects choose to sing hymns and go into longer durations of prayer before the ritual closing.

The ritual is closed as thus: "Hail Belial. Lord and Master of Earth. We thank thee for being present at our ritual. We bid you, go in peace."

Close the ritual as normal. If practicing solitary - change all "we" to "I" Also - the prayer can be done with a single candle if you lack the space, time, or supplies to do a drawn out ritual.

## Basic Rite To Lucifer

The Altar must face the East most point of the ritual chamber. A candle is set at each elemental point. The elemental Demons are invoked by use of the enns with the dagger. Invoke Flereous first and work clockwise, leaving Lucifer for last. An incense of Sorcery invokes atmosphere.

Light the candles from Flereous to Lucifer. Then - Carrying an incense wand or burner in one hand and a dagger in the other (doesn't matter which) approach each point and kneel reciting the enn for Lucifer and wave the dagger through the smoke. Finally, invite the fifth element (Satan, spirit) from the center of the ritual space.

Kneel at the altar in prayer: "We pray thee Lucifer, bestow upon us the strength of your design. Let the eagle bring us a new understanding. Your light shall be our protection and guide us through this life. We are as the wind. We humbly pay homage to thee in our offer of incense that you may know our respect for your vast strength. We offer requests of knowledge and reflection that we may employ your creation to do so. Hail Lucifer. Lord and Master of Air."

Then comes the typical ritual body in which requests of concentration, knowledge, intellect, and purification are burned at the altar. (i.e. a bowl, incense burner, or bonfire.) The ashes must be crushed to a fine powder and later dispersed in the wind. Some sects choose to sing hymns and go into longer durations of prayer before the ritual closing.

The ritual is closed as thus: "Hail Lucifer. Lord and Master of Air. We thank thee for being present at our ritual. We bid you, go in peace."

Close the ritual as normal. If practicing solitary - change all "we" to "I" Also - the prayer can be done with a single candle if you lack the space, time, or supplies to do a drawn out ritual.

## Basic Rite To Flereous

The Altar must face the South most point of the ritual chamber. A candle is set at each elemental point. The elemental Demons are invoked by use of the enns with the dagger. Invoke Leviathan first and work clockwise, leaving Flereous for last. An incense of sandalwood and sage invokes atmosphere.

Carrying a candle in one hand (doesn't matter which) approach each point and kneel reciting the enn for Flereous and lighting the candle. Finally, invite the fifth element from the center of the ritual space.

Kneel at the altar in prayer: "We pray thee Flereous, bestow upon us the strength of your design. Allow our actions to be swift and unfailing. Be present that our enemies will not conquer us. We are as flames burning brightly in your radiance. We humbly pay homage to thee in our offer of incense and fire that you may know our respect for your vast strength. We offer requests of vengeance and love that we may employ your creation to do so. Hail Flereous. Lord and Master of Fire."

Then comes the typical ritual body in which requests of vengeance and love are burned within the altar or primary ritual space fire. (i.e. a bowl, incense burner, or bonfire.) Some sects choose to sing hymns and go into longer durations of prayer before the ritual closing.

The ritual is closed as thus: "Hail Flereous. Lord and Master of Fire. We thank thee for being present at our ritual. We bid you, go in peace."

Close the ritual as normal. If practicing solitary - change all "we" to "I" Also - the prayer can be done with a single candle if you lack the space, time, or supplies to do a drawn out ritual.

## Basic Rite To Leviathan

The Altar must face the West most point of the ritual chamber. A candle is set at each elemental point. The elemental Demons are invoked by use of the enns with the dagger. Invoke Belial first and work clockwise, leaving Leviathan for last. An incense of Calamus and Frankincense invokes atmosphere.

Light the candles from Belial to Leviathan. Then - Carrying a Chalice of water (with sea salt) in one hand and a dagger in the other (doesn't matter which) approach each point and kneel reciting the enn for Leviathan and dip the dagger into the water and sprinkle it above each candle. Finally, invite the fifth element from the center of the ritual space.

Kneel at the altar in prayer: "We pray thee Leviathan, bestow upon us the strength of your design. Let the serpent wise deal death to the lies of our enemies. Allow our empathy to be our protection. Allow our anger to be swift with justice. Be present that our enemies will not conquer us. We are as the swift flowing tide ebbing to and fro. We humbly pay homage to thee in our offer of sea salt and water that you may know our respect for your vast strength. We offer requests of healing and emotional balance that we may employ your creation to do so. Hail Leviathan. Lord and Master of Water."

Then comes the typical ritual body in which requests of healing and emotional balance are burned within the altar or primary ritual space fire. (i.e. a bowl, incense burner, or bonfire.) Use the remaining water to put out the fire once the requests have been burnt. The ashes must be crushed to a fine powder and later dispersed in running water (i.e. ocean, stream). Some sects choose to sing hymns and go into longer durations of prayer before the ritual closing.

The ritual is closed as thus: "Hail Leviathan. Lord and Master of Water. We thank thee for being present at our ritual. We bid you, go in peace."

Close the ritual as normal. If practicing solitary - change all "we" to "I" Also - the prayer can be done with a single candle if you lack the space, time, or supplies to do a drawn out ritual.

## Rite to Baalberith & Eurynomous

This rite shall be done on the evening of October the 31st between the hours of 8pm and 2am November 1st. The person conducting the rite shall not eat or smoke or engage in sexual intercourse 12 hours minimum prior to the commencement of the rite.

*Preparation - you need:*

- red or black light for the ritual chamber (atmospheric)
- chalices
- bowls or incense burners
- charcoal
- black candles for the altar and all four elemental points
- sword for evocation
- Oleum of Baalberith or Eurynomous or both
- Oleum of Lucifuge Rofocale
- controlling oil
- 2x2 pieces of parchment
- melted black wax
- cup ground sage
- cup ground mullein
- ground mandrake root
- urine
- blood

*To Make Black Paper Squares for Rite Requests and Prayers*

Take 2x2 pieces of paper and soak in controlling oil for 10 minutes. Put paper on a cookie sheet, heat oven to low bake, bake for five minutes, let cool. place one at a time in melted black wax using a tweezer until fully covered. On one side of each place the sigil of Eurynomous or Baalberith. Store in a dark, dry box.

Oleum of Lucifuge Rofocale

> 1 cup olive juice - black
> 1 tsp olive oil (optional)
> 1/2 cup alcohol
> a pinch of ground mandrake
> a pinch of ground mullein

*Controlling Oil -*
Calamus root steeped in light vegetable oil.

*Incense*

> sage
> mandrake
> mullein
> 1 tsp of Lucifuge Rofocale Oleum

This rite is particularly useful for cursing and banishing negativity. This is the prelude to the Rite of Belial, which is the "New Beginning."

Use all black candles for elemental points. You may use a personal "power" candle of any color you choose on your altar if you choose. Place a chalice of sea salt mixed with water at each point (or water directly from the ocean). You may choose to have two chalices on the altar. One for the libation to Leviathan and one for the ceremonial drink/offering to the death Demons. You should also place bowls of dirt on top of which charcoal should be placed for the ritual incense - at each of the elemental points and one on the altar for burning requests. Your altar should face either your elemental point or the northwest point of your circle.

***IMPORTANT NOTE** - as you mix the salt and water with the dagger you must say the following for each chalice you mix –

### *"Talot pasa oida Belial et Leviathan"*

Invite the elemental Demons as you normally would by employing their enns. Invite Satan from the center using the following enn: "Ave Satanis! Tasa reme laris Satan."

From the Northmost point you will invite both Baalberith and Eurynomous.

To invite Balberith employ the enn - "Avage secore on ca Baalberith."

To invite Eurynomous employ the enn - " Ayar secore on ca Eurynomous."

Then recite the prayer (or use one of your own if you prefer) -

"Into this circle I welcome death. Of Baalberith and Eurynomous come forth and be present. For this ritual is in your honor. This night you reign supreme. I pray you to assist me in my workings and to bless this rite."

Now is the time for either silent prayer or to make requests. On the black paper squares you write your request, one letter over another, focusing your energy on the square. Hold the square over the flame before burning and recite the appropriate verse depending on intention. For group Rites - each person writes and burns her own requests.

**Cursing** - "Blanae core sanada. Recta sabra naca Flereous."

**Dispelling Negativity** - "Poco tasa helna rabac tasa. Recta sabra naca Flereous."

Burn all requests. The rite is then closed in the usual manner. The ashes of the requests and the remaining wax from the candle is buried (within 24 hours) in the ground. As you are burying the remains of the ritual you must say:

***"Padar ast fo ehaoth pedar ganabel Berith."***

Some people prefer to bury the requests in a graveyard. This is very symbolic not only from the cursing or death aspect, but also from the new beginnings aspect.

## Honoring the Ancestors – The Ancestral Altar

One of the many Demonolatry traditions is to erect a yearly altar to the anscestors during the month of Rite to Eurynomous. Upon this altar, place pictures of those who have died. Burn Eurynomous incense, and prayer candles on it. Place a sigil of Eurynomous, Baalberith, and Babaal upon it. Drape it in a black altar cloth. It doesn't need to be large or foreboding. It can be a small table that you can kneel before. On nights that you feel drawn to the altar, light a prayer candle and the incense and say a prayer for those deceased persons or pets who are pictured or whose items are sitting upon the altar. The point is to honor those who came before us, and the Demons who rule over death and change. Placing statues of Set or Anubis upon altars like this is also common.

## The Rites of Belphegore
This article was first published in Black Serpent, Spring 2006.

The Rites to Belphegore happen on March 31, April 9th, and May 13th. Traditionally these rites were celebrated to welcome the coming of new earth (Spring). It is common practice to have large feasts during these rites. It is said that if the Demonolator allows a few drops of his/her blood to fall upon the ground around these dates, Belphegore and the other earth-based Daemons will look kindly upon the practitioner for an entire year. Magick for new jobs, letting go of the past, stability, and help with mundane issues (i.e. finding a new place to live, house blessings etc...) can be done during the Rites to Belphegore.

Belphegore/Belphegor – has been a Demon of discovery, invention, riches, and sloth (one of the deadly sins). Originally an Assyrian God, Baal Poer, he ruled over lust. In Kabbalistic writings he was the opposite polarity of the sixth Sephiroth. He is an Earth Daemon. In the Dukante Hierarchy he is listed as a weapons master, a war daemon, and a daemon to be called on for gain in the material world.

# Nine Rites

Nine Rites are not much different than a regular rite except instead of invoking the elementals and Satan, all nine Divinities are invoked. There are two different ways to construct the ritual space – a traditional ritual circle, and a pyramid (triangle). Once again, let me reiterate that Pyramid rites should only be performed by experienced magicians because the energy is so erratic and strong that it can cause nausea, dizziness, vomiting, and even fainting.

The following is from one of the family Purswell grimoires/journals, Wales 1638. It describes how the Nine Divinities act together. My notes from transcription are noted by [ ]. I have included it, with permission, to give you a flavor of how Demonolators over time have viewed the nine Divinities.

*In Daemon's names be they Lucifer and Flereous adjacent* [looks like adjacent, but could not make out the word] *Leviathan and Belial. Encompassed all by Satan who is the source of all.*

*This, our holy kingdom of earth governed by the imperial hierarchy is terra, the earth. She is the womb of Unseré, whose consort is Satan. Mother of Belial, the solid earth whose element is solid matter. Lucifer, the light bringer indulges us in knowledge and brings us Flereous, the fire and warmth. Leviathan is the fertile seed whose waters breath life. Eurynomous brings death in the cycle [of regeneration, renewal]. Verrine heals of illness and disease. Amducious destroys in anger. United, nine stand in divinity. There are two of each element and the whole. Leviathan Unsere, Flereous Amducious, Belial Eurynomous, Lucifer Verrine, and Satan.* [I am perplexed by this division as I've never seen or considered it. I would have thought Verrine to be Water and Unsere Earth. But that would require Eurynomous to be Air, which makes no sense to me.] *Divided by three they are trinity. Leviathan Unsere Verrine, Eurynomous Amducious Flereous, Belial Lucifer Satan.* [Life, Death/Destruction, and Enlightenment/Knowledge]

[The] *Beginning of this cycle is the equinox, spring governed by Lucifer. Lucifer is youth whose naivety renews all and brings new knowledge. Ronove* [Ronwe] *is the wise mentor of this knowledge and stands to disperse it. Now is the time for the apprentice to take his place before the altar to receive the wisdom of the daemons.* [Initiation] *The altar stands before the North with its entrance East. Torches doth illuminate the outer boundary at each point where the elementals preside. Tasa Raimie Laris Satan, I ask thee forth to bear witness. This Rite is in honor of your son, Lucifer, Renich Tasa Uberaca Biasa Icar Lucifer! We pray thee bring light of your wisdom. We seek illumination to discover the mysteries of your creation. In that we discover the universe and our purpose on this plane. Come forth Flereous - Ganic Fubin Flereous and be present, we pray thee.*

# Diagrams of Ritual Layout

## Pyramid (triangle):

# Diagram of Altar Facing West

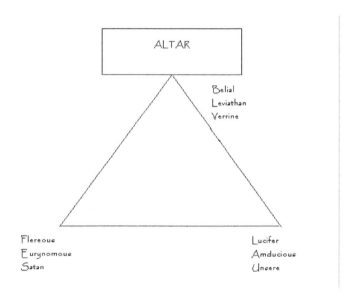

This is not the only configuration that can be used. For example, all of the more "destructive" Demons can be put together (Amducious, Flereous, Eurynomous), the creation Demons put together (Unsere, Verrine, Leviathan), and all the the enlightenment Demons put together (Lucifer, Belial, Satan).

**Circles using the nine** (the top being Earth):

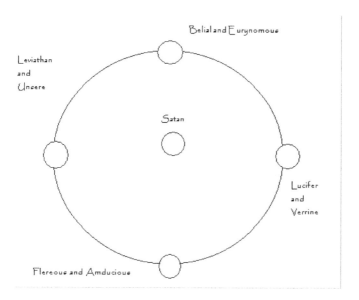

This particular circle is elemental. However, you can also choose polarity in which Lucifer and Leviathan would be in the East, Belial and Flereous in the North, Unsere and Amducious in the South, and Verrine and Eurynomous in the West. Or any combination thereof. In the case of Circles of Nine, Satan is always invoked from the center OR He can be invoked at every elemental point.

# Demonolatry Rites of Birth, Marriage, and Death

The following rites are very basic. These rites may vary from group to group or Demonolator to Demonolator, but the basic construction is the same. They can be modified as you wish. Please note that during any rite that asks you to fast that *fasting is optional*. Persons with medical conditions wherein fasting is not an option should not fast at all, or should not for any longer than you might fast for a blood draw. Usually 8-12 hours. Make sure you drink plenty of liquids during the fast.

## The Baptism

From literary allusions to metaphoric usage, the Baphometic Fire Baptism has come to symbolize the infinite rebirth of consciousness. In reality, for adult baptismal rites, this is truly the case. There is a definite difference between the adult baptism and the child baptism rites. For children, no blood is extracted and no marks are burnt into the skin. For adult rites, however, the baptismal rite does involve a small amount of pain.

The rite is opened as usual. However, at the center of the ritual chamber or space there is a circle painted with the sigils of each elemental Demon and that of Satan marking their corresponding points. At the center of the circle is the sigil of either the Sect Demon if the recipient is a child, or if the recipient of the ritual is an adult - the patron/matron Demon. In cases where a patron/matron has not been chosen the Sect Demon's sigil is used. Around this circle are many candles. White candles are traditional.

Once the circle has been constructed the baptism recipient, if an adult, is asked to give a few drops of blood, and if it is a child the parents are asked to give drops of their blood. The blood is mixed with the consecrated (blessed by Lord Leviathan) water on the altar for later use during the rite. The recipient of the ritual shall wear traditional robes of white, gray, or black.

The Adult Baptism - The person to be baptized stands inside the circle of candles as it is closed. It should be wide enough to allow the person to safely stand inside it with at least a foot on all sides to prevent robes or cords from catching fire. It is always best to keep extra water on hand and a fire extinguisher as a precaution. The candles are then lit. The following (or a variation thereof) is said by the presiding priest/ess over the person -

"Hail our infernal Lord, Satan. Hail [Sect Demon or Matron/Patron name]."

The enns of these Demons are then spoken.

"Blessed in the name of our Lord Satan is [name of person being baptized], your beloved child. By the North our Lord Belial, may she know her path. By the East our Lord Lucifer may she know her spirit. By the West our Lord Leviathan may she know her emotions. By the South our Lord Flereous may she know desire. By Baphomet may her path lead her to wisdom. All of this in the name of our Lord Satan and our Lord [presiding Demon] let it be known that this (wo)man is kindred among you and all those present this night. May she walk her path in Lucifer's Light. So be it."

At this time a pitcher of consecrated water is poured over the circle of candles until all flames are extinguished. The presiding priesthood opens the circle and leads the recipient to the altar. At this time the priest mixes the appropriate oleums with the blood water and anoints the recipient. [10]Then the branding iron is removed from the fire and the recipient bares her upper left thigh to receive the mark of either the Sect Demon or the Matron/Patron. Once marked the remaining water mixture is discarded to the soil and the rite is closed.

The Child Baptism - If the child is old enough to stand inside the circle quietly by herself she may. However, if the child is young it is best that one parent enter the circle, and hold the child or stand next to the child. The ritual proceeds as normal, however instead of the child's blood, the parents' blood is used and the child is not branded, but is anointed. Most Sects require both parents' permission to baptize a child (defined as any person under

---

[10] Some Sects choose to 'cut' the sigil in the flesh to produce a lighter scar. The problem with this method is the sigil must be redone every so often so that the mark does not fade. Some Demonolators have rectified the situation altogether by having the appropriate sigil tattooed on the left thigh instead.

the age of 18). Some already baptized children choose to have the ceremony re-done once they are old enough to undergo the full adult baptism ritual.

## The Marriage Ceremony

Demonolatry weddings can range from simple to complex. The following is the basic rite outline. It can be embellished to the required decorative or symbolic complexity, as the bride and groom require. As a standard this rite is done before the Coven/Sect and those not initiated are required to stand outside the circle and to the back. There is no exception for parents or relatives in most Sects. Other Sects are more lenient. There is no sect law stating homosexual couples cannot be joined with these rites.

The two things needed are the unity candle[11] and the binding cord. Most people choose red or blue for the unity candle. The binding cord is merely a piece of cord approximately 24 inches in length. Its color most often corresponds with the color of the unity candle and is kept by the couple after the ceremony ends.

The circle is constructed as usual. The altar faces the North[12]. The groom stands at the Southmost point of the circle and awaits his bride. The assisting ritual attendants bring her to him and they make their way down the center of the circle to the altar before the presiding priest. The Demon invited to this rite is Rosier. This enn is spoken and both bride and groom kneel before the altar.

---

[11] It is often misconstrued that the unity candle is a Christian concept. The practice dates from early pagan rites and is currently used in many different faiths and cultures during marriage ceremonies. The flame represents eternity and the element fire rules emotion and love. Hence its appropriate symbolism during the union of two people.

[12] Most of the time the direction the altar faces depends on the Demon presiding over the rite. That aside, the traditional direction for the altar to face is east. In the marriage rite the altar faces North to signify the new life the bride and groom will be beginning together.

The priest(ess) speaks the following or a variation thereof:

"Our Lord Rosier gathers us here to witness and rejoice in this union of [bride name] and [groom name]. Truly blessed is this day. Before all present and our Lord Satan these people wish to bind in love and matrimony for the rest of their days on this earth."

Bride and groom stand and join hands and the priest(ess) wraps the cord around their wrists binding them to one another while saying:

"Jedan Olmec Ayran, Rosier. Liran fortes Satanas."

The Coven/Sect resounds with : "Hail Rosier. Bind them and keep them in Love. We pray you."

The bride and groom (still bound as they will remain the rest of the rite) each offer several drops of blood, which is added to the ceremonial wine blessed by Lord Leviathan. Then they are each given a small white candle. They each light their candle from the center altar candle and together - ignite the unity candle. The flames of the lighting candles are extinguished in the water chalice. If any vows or speeches or sermons are to be made it is done at this time.

Once this is done the groom takes the wine chalice and presents it to his bride who takes the cup. "In the name of Rosier I drink to our everlasting union." She drinks and hands the chalice back to her groom who says the same, drinks, and returns the chalice to the altar.

The presiding priest(ess) then takes a small lock of both the bride and groom's hair and places it in a vial along with a small amount of the wine. The consecrated water is poured over the couple's bound hands and they are asked to turn toward the east.

The priest(ess) says: "In the eyes of our Lord Rosier and of our Lord Satan and in witness of all present, you are now wed until which time our Lords see it fit for you to part. Go to the East and Lucifer shall light your way. It is done."

The vial, now capped and its contents sealed is given to a trusted family member or friend for safe keeping. For there is a rite to undo a marriage and the vial will be needed if the couple wishes to part or if one partner dies and the other wishes to re-marry. If the vial is lost no other binding of love will be successful.

The couple keeps the cord and the remaining unity candle as mementos of the occasion. A reception follows.

## The Funeral

Addressed here is the age old question "What happens when we die?" While most Demonolators admit they are not positive what happens after death (if anything) many believe our souls transcend or move on. In a nutshell, reincarnation is a widespread belief among the Demonolatry community. However, it is not viewed quite like the esoteric "I was Cleopatra in a past life", but rather as ascending a ladder. It does not matter who we were, but who we will become. Each life has the potential to lead us closer to being reborn on the Demonic plane. So does this mean we become Demons? No. We go back to the elements from whence we came and are reborn from those same elements. Eventually a part of us will end up there. Of course this is only one view-point. Others believe our consciousness merely dies when we do. All the same, the fact remains that we return to the elements and therefore to the Demons. The Demonolatry Funeral rite reflects this philosophy.

Because of this cremation is usually chosen over burial. Also, because it is illegal in most U.S. States to scatter the remains of a dead person over pristine soils or in water many Demonolators have chosen to buy into their Coven/Sect crypt or to purchase a private family mausoleum for their urn. Not so strangely it does seem odd for a Demonolatry funeral rite to take place in a crematorium/funeral home chapel (even though this has been known to occasionally happen) so most rites are done at a family home after the cremation.

The circle is constructed as always. Selected items of the deceased are taken to the altar along with the urn. Eurynomous, Baalberith, and Babael are invited to preside during the rite. In a large bowl the deceased's items are placed. Each of the family members and friends write their farewells prior to the rite and bring them with them to burn during the ceremony. Most of the rite is done in silence to allow the mourners to reflect and mourn.

Each note/farewell is taken and burnt to ash and poured over the items, which will be buried or entombed with the ashes of the deceased. As each piece of paper is burnt the priest(ess) says: "By Flereous your spirit is lifted. Sanctified in the sacred flames you shall rise."

The incense is lit and waved over the altar. "By Lucifer your spirit settles softly to return to Belial."

Sand is poured into the bowl until everything is covered. "By Belial you become one with him. His ground, now desolate and seemingly barren, shall rebirth you."

Over that a chalice of consecrated water is poured. "By Leviathan your spirit is re-birthed in the elements."

The sigil of the Patron/Matron Demon is traced with the ritual dagger over the bowl. "May [patron/matron name] guide you and keep you."

"In the name of our Lord Satan it is done. We bid you farewell our brother/sister [name]."

Eulogies are done at this time if needed. The Priest(ess), assistants, and family members all take the urn and the bowl to the cemetery or burial place and entomb or bury the urn with the contents of the bowl and seal it. The outside of the tomb is anointed with the appropriate oleums and sigils.

# Demonolatry Magick

## Positive Workings

### Banishment/Purification

It is doubtful most Demonolators will ever need this ritual. Sometimes, however, we bring something nasty upon our ritual space that just won't go away on its own. If you find yourself having to perform banishings often - seek out a priest or priestess to find out what it is you're doing wrong during your ritual workings. You may be bringing nasty energy on yourself due to emotional or psychological problems. As always, **you should never practice intense ritual work if you are experiencing emotional or psychological discord.**

Make sure you have a large incense bowl if this is a large area. Burn Garlic (whole cloves) and Frankincense.

Call on the elemental Demons using the Demonic enns. -
Use the sword to conjure by drawing a D with a Z through
it as you recite the enns.

North - Lirach tasa vefa wehlc Belial
East - Renich tasa uberace biasa icar Lucifer
South - Ganic tasa fubin Flereous
West - Jedan tasa hoet naca Leviathan

Mix water and pure solar sea salt in a chalice. Use a dagger
to disperse the water across the area while saying:

"Malevolent spirits leave this place. In the names of Belial,
Lucifer, Flereous, and Leviathan - I command thee ...
retreat from whence you came."

Pour the remainder of the water/salt into the center of the
area.

Continue with a protection rite of your choice or any other
positive ritual working. To dismiss the Demons hold the
sword before you, kneel on the right knee and say at each
elemental point-

North - We thank thee Belial. Go in peace.
East - We thank thee Lucifer. Go in peace.
South - We thank thee Flereous. Go in peace.
West - We thank thee Leviathan. Go in peace.

This should close whatever malevolent force is at work in
this place.

## Elemental Balancing Ritual

As always, be reminded that Demonic Magick relies on two things: A. Demons B. The Natural Elements that make up our universe.

It is important to remember that healing rituals are no different. Water is the element of healing. Leviathan is the lord of water. His colors are blue, gray, and sometimes white.

Why we get sick - all sickness is caused by mental strains/stresses and environmental influences. We get sick when these things become negative. This is called an Elemental Imbalance. It is, essentially what it says. Your body becomes imbalanced and thus unhealthy.

To negate and correct the effects of the imbalance -- you must do, on a regular basis, what is commonly known as an Elemental Balancing Ritual.

This ritual relies heavily on creative visualization.

Set up your altar as you normally would, invoke your elemental Demonic circle, and sit comfortably in front of it. Some people prefer to do this ritual skyclad (naked) as opposed to robed.

First you must remove all of your elements from you. Do this by imagining you are holding a box. Into this box you put all of your elements, one at a time, and then throw the box from you. You may have to fill the box with each element more than once. Imagine Earth as soil and leaves. Imagine air as smoke. Fire and Water etc...

Once you have removed all your elements - and you will be able to tell because you will be exhausted-- you can begin replenishing that which you have freed yourself of. Imagine refilling the box with "fresh" elements. Only fill the box once with each element. Pull the box into you. When this is done correctly you will feel invigorated and energetic. Then you close the ritual as you normally would.

*Interesting Note:* This ritual can also be modified for different belief systems or to a personal belief system. I have been told it works just as well regardless of which gods you invoke if any.

**Figuring Out Your Elemental Makeup and Identifying Imbalance:**

You start out by taking your natal chart (You can get a free one at **www.alabe.com**) and looking at which signs you have in the twelve houses. Then you add them up based on element. Now that is only an indicator of where elemental imbalances might occur, and you might get imbalances that don't coincide with your chart due to whatever you may be doing. For example, expending too much energy on the emotional can either deplete water or cause you to build an excess of water. It's different for different people.

- **Aries** (FIRE)
- **Taurus** (EARTH)
- **Gemini** (AIR)
- **Cancer** (WATER)
- **Leo** (FIRE)
- **Virgo** (EARTH)
- **Libra** (AIR)
- **Scorpio** (WATER)
- **Sagittarius** (FIRE)

- **Capricorn** (EARTH)
- **Aquarius** (AIR)
- **Pisces** (WATER)

**Air Imbalance** – An air imbalance might have symptoms of trouble catching one's breath, thinking too much instead of doing, or not being able to think clearly.

**Fire Imbalance** – A fire imbalance may be identified by lack of motivation, exhaustion, being quick to anger, irritable, or extremely thirsty.

**Water Imbalance** – Water imbalances can be identified by extreme thirst, severe emotional mood swings, and the inability to go beyond feelings to find reason.

**Earth Imbalance** – Characteristics of an earth imbalance could include feeling lethargic, tired, and overly pessimistic.

If your chart is heavy in certain elements and light in others, it might be best to do regular balancing to help with a natural imbalance. For those of us who are naturally more balanced based on more balanced charts, an imbalance will be easier to identify.

## Ritual to ease the Common Cold/Flu/Depression

Demons Invoked: Verrier and Verrine, Demons of health and healing.

Elements Concentrated On: Fire and Water, the cleansing elements.

**Tools Needed**: Blue, Red, or Gray candles to embody the ritual participants illness, black candles for the altar to absorb the negative sickness energy, sword for casting the circle, parchment, ink and writing instrument, small satchel that you can wear around your neck after the ritual (color of your choice), and Calamus based incense. Some occult stores will sell a good healing incense so you do not have to make your own. Many people like making their own because they know what's in it. You will also need a vial of fresh water from a running river or rain water. And a large bowl in which you can burn something.

**What to do**: Cast the circle. Invoke Verrier and Verrine by calling on them and inviting them to be present during the ritual. Light the incense. Inscribe your name into the candle using a dagger or other sharp object. Anoint the candle with the water. Cut the palm of your hand to draw a few drops of blood. (A note about blood rituals - if you can re-open an old wound - do it or, if you're a woman, use menstrual blood.) Anoint the candle also with your blood. Light it.

**More creative visualization** - We only use 10% of our brains. The mind has to power to heal. Even faster still is the mind's ability to heal at a faster rate with the aid of Demonic entities. Sit in front of the altar and take deep breaths. Deep breathing allows the body to expel negative energies from it. Find the source of the illness. Perhaps your flu started in the stomach. This is where you should go. Close your eyes and imagine the cleansing element absorbing into and permeating that part of your body and slowly moving throughout until you are radiating the color of the element you chose to cleanse you.

**The Request** - Take a deep breath. At the altar - write your request for health onto the piece of parchment. Place the sigils of Verrier and Verrine upon it along with your own signature. Burn the request by lighting it first with the left altar candle, then the right, then the center candle. Allow it to burn within the bowl. When the fire has fully devoured the parchment, mix in incense and the remaining wax from the candle once it has burnt down. Place all of this in the sachet and anoint with water. Wear around the neck until health is restored.

## The Rite of Ronwe

To aid in study and matters of an intellectual nature

Items Needed:

- Yellow Candle
- Wine in a Chalice

Invoke the elemental circle. Light a yellow candle and call on Ronwe with the Enn. - *"Kaymen Vefa Ronwe."*

Then say (and you can translate it into any language you feel comfortable with) - "I call on thee, Ronwe. Be present. Help me to gain concentration and wisdom. Help me to learn that which I have yet to learn. I invite you as my teacher. Ave Ronwe."

Relax and sip your wine. Remain conscious of your surroundings and your goals and be sure to set your expected goal firmly in your mind. Once the candle is burnt about 1/4 the way down - pull out your books and study or concentrate on the matter at hand. Sometimes it also helps if the practitioner plays mood music in the background. Instrumental is good.

Burning a vanilla or sandalwood incense will also help further relax you.

## A Demonolatry Rite to Make a Pet a Familiar
### ~Delepitorae

a mold of some sort
pet's hair/scales
your own hair/nail clippings/blood
dragons blood oil
candle of your element

Construct circle. Light altar candles. Your pet must be in the room with you. Light your elemental candle. In the mold place a bit of the pet's hair or scales mixed with your own hair, clippings, or blood. Take your elemental candle and drip the wax from it into the mold. While doing this place the dragon's blood and mix it into the mold also. Once it dries, pop it out of the mold and carve the sigil of your patron Demon into it. Allow your pet to touch and see it. Keep this item on your altar or in a safe place.

# Negative Rites & Workings

## Curses and Other Such Workings[13]
*From Dukanté's Book of fire.*

*A note about curses:* Do not feel guilt or remorse before, during, or after doing a curse and make sure you have thought about the curse for three days before performing it so there is less of a chance for guilt or remorse. If you feel guilt or remorse, you will oftentimes bring back on yourself that negativity you put out. In essence, you curse yourself. So make sure you are 100 percent sure and that the person you are cursing genuinely deserves it.

Also, do not confuse curses with spells. A curse alone is usually not done as a rite in and of itself in Demonolatry but it is always done within the confines of a ritual circle for a balance of energy. Also, I have not drawn rites around them within this book for the simple fact that rewriting the base rite would make for trite and tedious reading. Each of these actions are to be done during rites dedicated to Demons of war and vengeance, or during the Rite to Eurynomous and Baalberith. Done alone or by themselves, outside a structured rite, these actions may not accomplish the desired end.

**For Revenge:** To control thy flame within you seek, light by spark and cease to speak. Thine hand of right to cast the spell, all set for ill and well. Mighty sword by the ring be sought, the elements thyself hath brought. Behold the rites of Belphegore and spill thy blood as this be sworn:

---

[13] First Printed as "From the Book of Fire: A Gallery of Curses and Other Workings," Transcribed and edited by S. Connolly.

"Avenged be, revenge be mine, my foe hath sought the path of blind."

To Seal thine words of this dismay - the sword to cast this Baphomet. Above thy flame of vengeance burn, identified with blazing stern. With this done and all hath said, add the dirt of one long dead.

**Vengeance Against People Who Are Two-Faced:** If foes be said or heard to cast hate toward others - be his face a mirror of time, cast the elements full of darkness, upon that which you stand. Banish deep into the ground a vial of junipers in a place where nothing grows. And hem thy robes with lockets of black and brown and gold. Within a stump- having been dead for thirteen moons, place black tapers with tongues of fire inscribed with Demonic runes.

Inscribe the seal of fire, Flereous you doth seek, upon a hide of bark, which on a curse be writ. Destroy the bark by fire to bring your opposer to halt and free thyself of torment.

**For a Friend Who Has Wronged You:** Capture the face of hate within a glass reflection and urinate upon it on putrid ground while chanting: "He who hath a double name be said to put himself to shame and I who bring this prophesy, cursed be mine enemy."

**To Be Rid of Someone You Dislike:** To be rid of those who crowd thy path, behold the earth of years long past. Along with Oleum of water mix within iron cast. A conqueror can build this wall, a sprig of birch with fire and stone. And with these words boil say: "Uva Rasar Hecate"

With focused images in thy mind, seek thine foe may he be blind. Protection thus, his be lost, gain to you at any cost.

**To Ruin a Friendship or Love Affair:** To those unite of own free will, the next be cast thy friendship ill. Of each element which they stake, a handful of each for which thou shalt take. Hemlock of earth, the ground much adorned. Hensbane for air, vengeance be sworn. Wolvesbane for fire, flame seek the night. Belladonna for water, destroy all sought light. Seek each out as a mighty hawk and place thy bane where they hath walk. By candlelight, the black be lit, upon parchment herein must be writ:

> Sanarin Serpenté
> Destroyer Serpenté
> Senarin Arei
> Destroyer Arei
> Senarin Erté
> Destroyer Erté
> Senarin Salmé
> Destroyer Salmé

Say: Salmé hath known me - I beseech thee, show thyself unto me.

With this invocation affirmed, the parchment shall then be burned. Ashes over distant ground to be hidden and never found.

**To Keep A Curse Until Needed:** Project thy energy doth you seek, thine element vastly wise. Upon its fury thus you speak the words bring forth demise: Darak Vana Evate, Seron Evna Evate.

And thus a flame be turned to red, a fury glow of blood. By thine hand, needle and thread the sigil must be done. An eagle with fire breath upon a sacred oak. A symbol of destruction, death - placed within putrid smoke. Between the bonds of black and white this seal you must keep. To keep the power bound up tight until it is released.

## Curse of the Demon Sonnillion (or Tezrian) (*The Blood Curse*)

- Materials Needed: One Black Candle
- Oleum of Sonnillion or Tezrian or other like vengeance Demon.
- Parchment and ink
- A bowl large enough for burning parchment
- Square of Red Cloth
- Sword or dagger.

Invoke the elemental circle. Then you must call upon Sonnelion from the South. Anoint the candle with the Oleum and inscribe the victims name on the candle and ignite it. Chant the Demonic enn. over the candle - "Ayar Serpente Sonnelion. Ater Salme Sonnelion. Ave Satanas."

Place the Sigil of Sonnelion onto the parchment. Beneath it, write the name of the person you swear vengeance upon. Fold the Parchment - pour Oleum over it - ignite it in the flame of the candle. Let it burn within the bowl. Allow the candle to burn down fully. Put the remaining wax into the bowl with the ashes of the sigil request. Cut your palm and allow three drops of your blood - or more - to mingle with the contents of the bowl.

Chant over the bowl thrice - "Avage secoré, ón ca Sonnelion."

Wrap the contents into a square of red cloth. Under a full moon, bury the parcel in a secluded place.

## The Cord Of Nine

Take a cord of leather to your ritual chamber along with a picture or like item belonging to or in the likeness of the enemy. Use a needle or dagger to prick the leather nine times while saying: Fair is foul, foul is fair, I throw this curse into the air, dark be black as darkness be, around this wretch so it shall be. A prayer cord used specifically for this type of rite is recommended.

## [14]Demonolatry Coriander Curse

Mix a cup of coriander (or black poppy) with a cup of salt and pass mixture from hand to hand before a fire while saying:

Salt and coriander I conjure thee.
By Lucifer, By Satanis,
By Flereous cursed be.
Not as salt and coriander I call thee,
But the heart of [VICTIM]

Toss the mixture into the fire and say:

As thou burnst, so let the heart of [VICITIM] burn
And bring it here to me!
Conjured by Unsere
By the underworld itself
and the serpents of the sea.
[VICTIM] I summon thee.
By Lucifer, By Satanis,

---

[14] A variation of this curse appears in Mastering Witchcraft by Paul Huson.

By Leviathan conjured be.
By the underworld itself
Unsere
Enter in [VICTIM]
And bring him here to me.
Powers of the elements
Bring him here to me!
With more messages I send to call thee.
By Unsere, Demoness of sorcery.
By Tezrian
Who walks the battlefields by day
and haunts the crossroads at night.
Spinning wars and enmity.
Take [VICTIM] to you
so that we may be freed of his mortal existence.

## Binding and Control

Soak in Calamus oil a parchment with the victims name and the sigil of Amducius written upon it. Soak a high john the conqueror root in a resin oil made from its own outer skin. Wrap the parchment around the root and bind with a purple cord or thread whilst saying: You are bound by Amducious.

## To Stop Gossip

Mix equal parts of Rue, Garlic, and Hensbane. Mix in a bit of your own urine. Put it in an envelope and mail it to the gossiper.

## To Part Lovers In The Name of Satan

Mix equal parts of urine, mandrake, mullein, hemlock, wormwood, and rose thorns. Construct a circle and have within it - 1 black candle. Inscribe the names of the lovers into the candle and let it burn down. Mix any remaining wax with the herbal mixture. Empower the mixture by chanting over it: "Qui Osa Satan Lila Fubine et Kalo." Toss the mixture into the yard or doorway of the places the victims live.

## To Let Leviathan Judge if an Enemy Has Wronged You

Amidst any rite you may call on Leviathan as such:
"By Leviathan. Great Lord of Water. I ask thee be present as to Judge this person who is named: [person's name]. I place my trust in you, wise serpent, and in your judgment and fairness. I ask that you [request] [victim's name] as (s)he has thrown my life into discord. Let all protective boundaries be taken from him/her. Yet protect me from harm as I respect the nature of your design and worship you thus."

## To Break a Curse Placed on You (To Forfeit a Symbol)

To turn a symbol of curse carved into, or put onto objects belonging to you by someone who would wrong you - go over the symbol with a dagger. Then complete it if it is incomplete. Rub Calamus oil over the symbol thus breaking the enemy's control and making it your own.

## Sleep of Sickness

Place a sigil of Verrine scribed backwards in blood between the enemy's mattress', beneath his bed, or sewn into his pillow cases. The victim will surly fall ill.

**A Working of Demonolatry to get a fellow co-worker into trouble. ~Delepitorae**

> tansy
> lichen (moss)
> garlic
> mullein
> rue

Powder these and sprinkle onto the victims locker or things while saying: GANIC IOD PAR LANIRE HESTA WITHAR SATAN.

# The Demonolatry Tree of Life and the Qlippoth

The Nine Demonic Divinities are the cornerstone of traditional Demonolatry practice. This article will delve deeper into the symbolism of the nine, and will give you several different perspectives of the symbolism as much of it can depend on the way the individual thinks and how that individual perception helps the individual along his or her personal path work.

The idea of the nine is nothing new. Nine has always been an important number dating back to the ancient Egyptians who were the first to herald nine as the number of foundation and balance. However, they honored ten different deities in their tree of life. In Demonolatry, technically we honor ten as well. The Nine Divinities and the Self.

But before we get to that, let's first go over who the Nine are, what they symbolize, and their elemental breakdowns according to some Demonolators.

Once again, the following are the **Nine Demonic Divinities**. They are repeated again and again because they are important. Memorize them.

**Satan**
**Lucifer**
**Flereous**
**Leviathan**
**Belial**
**Verrine**
**Amducious**
**Unsere**
**Eurynomous**

Next, we'll again list their purpose, Enn, Rituals, Seasons, and how some Demonolators have seen them and corresponded them. That way you don't have to flip around the book to reference them for this section.

- *Satan* - King : *Tasa reme laris Satan - Ave Satanis* - Direction: Center/All ; Color: All ; Months: All ; Seasons All ; Rituals- Any.; Satan appears as a sage wise man with silver hair and black eyes. His eyes have been described as seeing nothing and seeing all. However their color or features are non-descript.
- *Lucifer* - Air Elemental : *Renich Tasa Uberaca Biasa Icar Lucifer* - Direction: East; Colors: White Yellow; Month: March; Season: Spring; Ritual: Enlightenment, spring equinox, initiations. Lucifer appears with long, black hair and blue eyes. His voice is considered average though he seems overly excited most of the time. He wears pendants of eagles. Twin to Lucifuge.

- ***Flereous*** - Fire Elemental : *Ganic Tasa Fubin Flereous* - Direction: South; Color: Red, Orange; Month: June; Season: Summer; Ritual: Baptism, action, love, solstice. Flereous appears as a tall man with long, red, course hair and red eyes. His voice is low and hissing. His expression is that of placidity.

- ***Leviathan*** - Water Elemental : *Jaden Tasa Hoet Naca Leviathan* - Direction: West; Colors: Blue, Gray; Month: September; Season: Autumn; Ritual: emotions, initiation, equinox, healing, fertility. Leviathan appears with long black hair and blue/gray eyes so striking it is as if you are staring into the waters of your own soul. His voice is low, his speech reserved. He is also shorter than Lucifer and Flereous, but stands a hair taller than Belial. He wears an amulet of his own sigil.

- ***Belial*** - Earth Elemental : *Lirach Tasa Vefa Wehlc Belial* - Direction: North; Colors: Green, Brown, Black; Month: December; Season: Winter; Ritual: initiation, new beginnings, winter solstice. Belial appears with hair colored black and white like salt and pepper (some people report his hair to be blonde). His eyes shift from brown to green. His voice comes off as being quite normal, though he speaks with resolute confidence in everything he says. He often seems perplexed or confused by some great mystery. He is not as tall as some of the other elementals.

- ***Verrine*** - Demon of Health : *Elan Typan Verrine* - Direction: Northwest; Colors: Blue, white; Month: November; Season: Late Autumn; Ritual: healing.

- ***Amducious*** - The destroyer : *Denyen valocur avage secore Amducious* - Twin to Asmodeous. Direction: Southeast. Colors: Orange; Month: May; Season: Late Spring; Ritual: war, action, dispel old.

- **Unsere** - (Female) Fertility and Sorcery : *Unsere tasa lirach on ca ayar* - Direction: Northeast; Colors: Green and White; Month: February; Season: Late Winter; Ritual: Wisdom, patience, motherhood.; Unsere has deep green eyes like the fertile plains of Ireland [Adrianna's note - I saw her with blue eyes]. Her hair is brown with strands of spun silver. Her eyes smile and sparkle. Her energy is gentle and nurturing. She travels often in a cowl-hooded cloak. Most memorable are her thin, delicate, pale hands. She dissolves as a mist. She is said to often appear to women during or after childbirth to breath life into infants. [Delaney Grimoire Reference]

- **Eurynomous** - Demon of Death : *Ayar Secore on ca Eurynomous* Direction: Northwest. Colors: Black and White; Month: October; Season: Late Autumn; Ritual: New beginnings, death, rebirth, celebration of death, Halloween. Eurynomous appears as a shadow or wraith. Or as a common man with white or translucent hair and pale or white eyes. His energy is calming and cool. He also holds the book of the dead. He often communicates vi baoith raimi Kairtey - or as invisible hands.

*From the Purswell Grimoires- Elemental Breakdown of the Nine*
Satan: All
Belial/Eurynomous - Earth
Lucifer/Verrine - Air
Flereous/Amducious - Fire
Leviathan/Unsere - Water

*From the Purswell Grimoires - Purpose Breakdown of the Nine*
Enlightenment: Lucifer/Belial/Satan

Creative: Leviathan/Unsere/Verrine
Destructive: Flereous/Amducious/Eurynomous

     These Nine are, indeed, the foundation or balance and can consequently be put into the tree of life (by my perspective) as such:

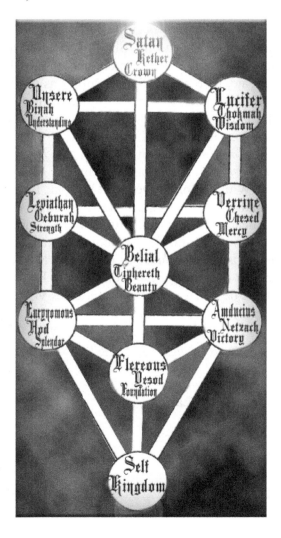

It is important to know that in the Tree of Life, the left pillar is Severity, the middle pillar is Mild (neutral), and the right pillar is that of Mercy.

My thinking behind placing the nine in this manner was thus: Flereous begins as the foundation, that special fire or light that we all come from. He leads to Eurynomous in the splendor of transformation from the actual physical consciousness to the spiritual physical consciousness, which leads to Amducious. Amducious is the physical warrior and the spiritual victory that leads to the perceived mental and emotional beauty that is Belial. Belial is the beauty of the physical and mental. He leads to Leviathan who represents emotional and mental strength and it is in that strength that we find Verrine, who is mercy. Mercy and Verrine in turn lead to Unsere and the feminine understanding. It is in understanding that we discover the masculine wisdom and ultimately a bond with the Divine – Satan.

It is also important to know that instead of considering there being two of each elemental as suggested in one of the listings aforementioned, I took an alchemical look at the Nine Divinities. Four were elemental and four became alchemical.

In my interpretation of the Nine, in regards to the Tree of Life, Flereous, Eurynomous, and Amducious represent the physical consciousness. Belial, Leviathan, and Verrine constitute the mental consciousness. And finally, Unsere, Lucifer, and Satan represent the spiritual consciousness.

**10. The Self (Malkuth, Kingdom).** We are the physical manifestations of the divine.

**9. Flereous (Yesod, Foundation)** is the foundation in fire. There would be no life without the sun or the desire for life. It is from fire, which our universe began. Therefore it is the foundation of life and an essential element. Fire also represents the desire. Desire for life, knowledge, and earthly pleasure.

**8. Eurynomous (Hod, Splendor)** is the splendor, earth transformed air (Dry). There is splendor in transformation and change of consciousness. Change is always severe, hence it's place on the pillar of Severity. Death equals the change from fire as in a mutable rebirth. The Baphometic Fire Baptism is the perfect example of this.

**7. Amducious (Netzach, Victory)** is air transformed fire (Heat), the victory over the physical emerges transformed victorious. It is the mastery of the physical will and over the limitations of the physical body. While Amducious may seem destructive, force is ruled by will whereas change happens regardless. Therefore just as Amducious can choose to be destructive, there is more power and strength in being able to will oneself toward mercy. Hence the reason Amducious sits on the pillar of Mercy.

**6. Belial (Tiphereth, Beauty)** is the beauty of Earth. In those things tangible as earth, Belial connects the physical to the mental bringing about an awareness of beauty for all things.

**5. Leviathan (Geburah, Strength)** is emotional and mental strength through water. In recognition of the physical and mental there is strength. Strength can be seen in the resistance of water. This leads to an emotional maturity necessary to move on to Verrine and mercy.

**4. Verrine (Chesed, Mercy)** is water transformed earth (Cold). From emotional stability and maturity comes strength of intuition, which leads to mercy and the recognition of that which needs to be healed. Healing the Self, and others, is merciful to the self and others.

**3. Unsere (Binah, Understanding)** is fire transformed water (Vapor/Steam). She leads to an understanding and feminine wisdom of the self and others. She is the connection from the mental to the divine/spiritual. This leads to enlightenment.

**2. Lucifer (Chokmah, Wisdom)** is air and wisdom. This enlightenment and wisdom is being able to see the whole in conjunction with the sum of its parts in order to reach gnosis.

**1. Satan (Kether, Crown)** is the source and the divine and consists of all elements and alchemical conjunctions and transmutations. He is the eternal spirit and the Divine.

We all start at 10 and work our way to 1 on our individual paths to spiritual enlightenment. Additionally, I felt this was important:

**Physical:**
Flereous is neutral and combined of the physical, mental, and spiritual. Eurynomous is feminine spiritual. Amducius is the masculine physical

**Mental**:
Belial is neutral and combined physical, mental, and spiritual. Leviathan is the feminine physical. Verrine is the masculine spiritual.

**Spiritual**

Satan is the neutral divine. Unsere is the feminine mental
Lucifer is the masculine mental

I tried to further break them down into positive negative,
but found that each of these Demons possess both positive
and negative aspects.

You may be wondering why I did not include Daath.
After discussing it over with others, we came to the
conclusion that Daath had to be Lucifuge Rofocale. See this
book's cover to discover Daath. He represents the spiritual
breath that connects the body to the mind to create the
whole of the physical manifestation of the Divine – Our
Selves.

- **Lucifage** - High Command (Control) : *Eyen tasa
  valocur Lucifuge Rofocale* His twin brother is
  Lucifer. Lucifuge is often seen as a father figure
  who gives sound advice and who is firm but often
  quiet.

But none of this is a new idea. Not by a long shot.
People have been working with nine far longer than
recorded history.

Many people believe the Tree of Life was a creation
from Jewish mysticism. The truth is it goes further back. In
the ancient pyramids of Egypt, the following was
discovered:

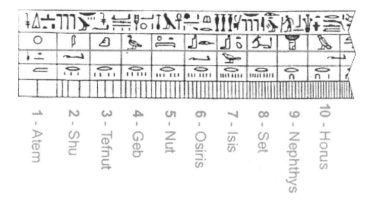

| | 1 - Atem | 2 - Shu | 3 - Tefnut | 4 - Geb | 5 - Nut | 6 - Osiris | 7 - Isis | 8 - Set | 9 - Nephthys | 10 - Horus |

Of which we can put into the tree of life as thus:

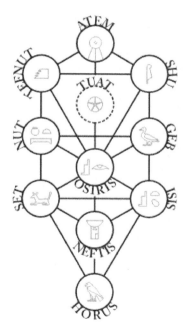

Notice that Atem is also the source of all, Kether, just as Satan.

It would also be difficult to discuss the Tree of Life without including the Qlippoth. The Qlippoth, also known as the Tree of Death, allegedly shows the opposite the Arch Angels. This is a very Christian viewpoint. Demonolators do not believe in black or white or good or evil. Therefore, this particular tree, as seen by many of us, is merely a difference in hierarchy and nothing more.

**THE SPHERES**

**1. URANUS**

**2. NEPTUNE**

**3. SATURN**

**4. JUPITER**

**5. MARS**

**6. SUN**

**7. VENUS**

**8. MERCURY**

**9. MOON**

**10. EDEN**

**DAATH - PLUTO**

| THE QLIPHOTH ARCH-DEMONS |
| --- |
| 1. SATAN (LUCIFER) & MOLOCH |
| 2. BEELZEBUB |
| 3. LUCIFUGE ROFACALE |
| 4. ASTAROTH |
| 5. ASMODEUS |
| 6. BELPHEGOR |
| 7. BAEL |
| 8. ADRAMELECH |
| 9. LILITH |
| 10. NAHEMA |
| CHARON? |

Please Note: This article first appeared in the Summer 2006 issue of Black Serpent and has been included in this book because it was worthy of inclusion as further exploration of the Nine Demonic Divinities.

# Modification of the Enochian Keys for Demonolatry

The keys were written by Dr. John Dee and Edward Kelley. Allegedly Dee got the keys from the angels themselves. There are 19 here (of the original 30). The keys have not been modified by much. I've simply replaced the name of Satan and/or specific Demons into places where the Christian God is referred to, or the concept of a particular Demon fits. The reason I have not changed them or taken other liberties is because I feel that each key contains an interesting Hermetic principle that each Adept student should contemplate.

The truth is the enochian keys spring from an older source. Many ceremonial magicians will smite me for saying this, but I believe Dee and Kelley did not get them from angels. Sorry. They are, in fact, more elaborate descriptions  -with liberties taken- of the Keys from the Corpus Hermetica.

Anton Szandor LaVey's liberal interpretation of the Enochian keys can be found in *The Satanic Bible*.

For the adept, meditate on these keys keeping in mind Hermetic principles and spiritual alchemy. You may see them differently.

## Key 1

I rayng over you, sayeth Satan, in power exalted above the firmaments of wrath: in whose hands the Sun is as a sword and the Moon as a through thrusting fire: which measureth your garments in the midst of my vestures, and thrust you together in the palms of my hands: whose seats are garnished with the fire of gathering, and beautified your garments with admiration. To whom I made a law to govern the Daemons and delivered you a rod with the ark of knowledge. Moreover you lifted up your voices and swear obedience and faith to Lucifer who brought light and whose beginning is not, nor end cannot be, which shineth as a flame in the midst of your palace, and reigneth amongst you as the balance of righteousness and truth. Move, therefore, and show yourselves: open the mysteries of your creation: Be friendly unto me: for I am a servant of Satan, the true worshipper of the Aether of all that is.

## Key 2

Can the wings of the wind understand your voices of wonder, O you the second of the first, whom the burning flames have framed within the depth of my jaws: whom I have prepared as cups for a wedding, or as the flowers in their beauty for the chamber of righteousness. Stronger are your feet than the barren stone, and mightier are your voices than the manifold winds. For you are become a building such is not, but in the mind of the all powerful. Arise, sayeth Ronwe: Move therefore unto Me: show yourselves in power: and make me a strong seething: for I am of Satan and liveth forever.

## Key 3

Behold sayeth Satan, I am a circle on whose hands stand 12 kingdoms: six are the seats of living breath: the rest are sharp sickles or the horns of death, wherein the creatures of your earth are to are not, except my own hand which sleep and shall rise. In the first I make you stewards and placed you in the 12 seats of government, giving unto every one of you power successively over 456, the true ages of time: to the intent that from your highest vessels and the corners of your governments you might work my power, pouring down the fires of life and increase continually on the earth: Thus you are become the skirts of Justice and Truth in the name of Amducious, lift up, I say, your selves. Behold his mercies flourish and name is become mighty amongst us. In whom we say: move, descend, and apply yourselves unto us, as unto the partakers of the Secret Wisdom of your creation

## Key 4

I have set my feet in the south and have looked about me, saying, are not the thunders of increase numbered 33 which reign in the second angle? Under whom I have placed 9639 whom none yet hath numbered but one, in whom the second beginning of things are wax strong, which also successively are the number of time: and their powers are as the first 456. Arise, Asmodeus and Flereous, and visit the earth: for I am Satan, and liveth. In the name of all that is, move and show yourselves as pleasant deliverers, that you may praise the Demonic Divine amongst the sons of men.

## *Key 5*

The mighty sounds have entered in your third angle and are become as olives in your olive mount, looking with gladness upon the earth and dwelling in the brightness of the heavens as continual comforters. Unto whom I fastened pillars of gladness 19 and gave them vessels to water the earth with her creatures: and they are the brothers of the first and second and the beginning of their own seats which are garnished with continual burning lamps 69636 whose numbers are as the first, the ends, and your contents of time. Therefore come you by the nature of your creation: visit us in peace and comfort: conclude us as receivers of your mysteries: for why? Our Lord and Master is all one. (Satan)

## *Key 6*

The spirits of the fourth angle are nine, mighty in the firmament of waters: whom the first hath planted a torment to the wicked and a garland to the righteous: giving unto them fiery darts to winnow the earth and 7699 continual workmen whose courses visit with comfort the earth and are in government and continuance as the second and the third. Wherefore harken unto my voice: I have talked of you and I move you in power and presence: whose works shall be a song of honour and the praise of Satan in your creation.

## *Key 7*

The East is a house of virgins singing praises amongst the flames of glory wherein Amducious hath opened his mouth: and they are become 28 living dwellings in whom the strength of man rejoices, and they are apparelled with ornaments of brightness such as work wonders on all creatures. Whose kingdoms and continuance are as the third and fourth strong towers and places of comfort, the seats of mercy and continuance. O you Demons of mercy: Move, appear: sing praises unto Satan and be mighty amongst us. For to this remembrance is given power and our strength waxes strong in our comforter.

## *Key 8*

The midday, the first, is as the third abyss made of hyacinth pillars 26: in whom the elders are become strong which I have prepared for my own sayeth Satan: whose long continuance shall be as bucklers to the stooping dragon and like unto the harvest of the widow. How many are there which remain in the glory of the earth, which are, and shall not see death, until this house fall and the dragon sink? Come away for the thunders have spoken: come away for the crowns of the temple and the coat of him that is Eurynomous, was, and shall be crowned, are divided. Come, appear to the terror of the earth and to our comfort and of such as are prepared.

## *Key 9*

A mighty guard of fire with two-edged swords flaming which have vials 8 of wrath for two times and a half: whose wings are of wormwood and off the marrow of salt, have settled their feet in the west and are measured with their ministers 9996. These gather up the moss of the earth as the rich man does his treasure: cursed are they whose iniquities they are in their eyes are millstones greater than the earth, and from their mouths run seas of blood: their heads are covered with diamond, and upon their heads are marble sleeves. Happy is he on whom they frown not. For why? Flereous rejoices in them! Come away and not your vials, for time is such as requires comfort.

## *Key 10*

The thunders of Judgement and Wrath are numbered and are harboured in the North in the likeness of an oak, whose branches are nests 22 of Lamentation and Weeping laid up for the earth, which burn night and day: and vomit out the heads of scorpions and live sulphur mingled with poison. These be the thunders that 5678 times in the 24th part of a moment roar with a hundred mighty earthquakes and a thousand times as many surges which rest not nor know any echoing time here. One rock brings forth 1000, even as a heart of man does his thoughts. Wo, wo, wo, wo, wo, wo, yea wo be to the earth! For Belial's iniquity is, was and shall be great. Come away: but not your noises.

## *Key 11*

The mighty sea groaned and they were 5 thunders which flew into the East: and the eagle spoke and cried with a loud voice, come away: the house of death of whom it is measured and it is as they are, whose number is 31. Come away, for I have prepared for you. Move, therefore, and show yourselves: open the mysteries of your creation: be friendly unto me: for I am the servant of Satan, the true worshipper of the highest.

## *Key 12*

O you that reign in the South and are 28, the lanterns of Sorrow, bind up your girdles and visit us. Bring down your train 3663 that Satan may be magnified, whose name amongst you is Asmodeus. Move, I say, and show yourselves: open the mysteries of your creation: be friendly unto me: for I am the servant of Satan, the true worshipper of the highest.

## *Key 13*

O you swords of the South which have 42 eyes to stir up the wrath of sin, making men drunken which are empty. Behold the promise Satan and his power which is called amongst you a bitter sting. Move, therefore, and show yourselves: open the mysteries of your creation: be friendly unto me: for I am the servant of Satan, the true worshipper of the highest.

## *Key 14*

O you sons of fury, the daughters of the Just, which sit upon 24 seats, vexing all creatures of the earth with age, which have under you 1636: behold the voice of Satan, the promise of Him which is called amongst you Fury or Extreme Justice. Move, therefore, and show yourselves: open the mysteries of your creation: be friendly unto me: for I am the servant of Satan, the true worshipper of the highest.

## *Key 15*

O thou the first governor of the first flame under whose wings are 6739 which know the great name Lucifuge and the Seal of Honour. Move, therefore, and show yourselves: open the mysteries of your creation: be friendly unto me: for I am the servant of Satan, the true worshipper of the highest.

### Key 16

O thou second flame, the house of Justice, which has your beginning in glory and shall comfort the Just: which walk the earth with feet 8763 that understand and separate creatures: great are thou Satanchia, Come Forth and Conquer. Move, therefore, and show yourselves: open the mysteries of your creation: be friendly unto me: for I am the servant of Satan, the true worshipper of the highest.

### Key 17

O thou third flame whose wings are thorns to stir up vexation and have 7336 lamps living going before you, whose God is Dagon, gird up thy loins and harken. Move, therefore, and show yourselves: open the mysteries of your creation: be friendly unto me: for I am the servant of Satan, the true worshipper of the highest.

### Key 18

O thou mighty light and burning flame of comfort which opens the glory Satan to the centre of the earth, in whom the secrets of truth 6332 have their abiding, which is called in thy kingdom Joy and not be measured: be thou a window of comfort unto me. Move, therefore, and show yourselves: open the mysteries of your creation: be friendly unto me: for I am the servant of Satan, the true worshipper of the highest.

### Key of the 30 Ayres

O you abyss, which dwell in the First Ayre, are mighty in the parts of the earth, and execute the judgement of the highest! To you it is said, behold the face of Satan, the beginning of comfort, whose eyes are the brightness of the heavens: which provided for you the government of the earth and her unspeakable variety, furnishing you with a power understanding to dispose all things according to the providence of Him that sits on the holy throne, and rose up in the beginning saying: the earth let her be governed by her parts and let there be division in her, that the glory of her may be always drunken and vexed in it self. Her course, let it run with the heavens, and as a handmaid let her serve them. One season let it confound with another, and let there be no creature upon or within her the same: all her members let them differ in their qualities, and let there no one creature equal with another: the reasonable creatures of the earth let them vex and weed out one another, and the dwelling places let them forget their names: the work of man, and his pomp, let them be defaced: his buildings let them become caves for the beasts of the field. Confound her understanding with darkness. For why? It repents me I made man. One while let her be known and another while a stranger: because she is the bed of a harlot, and the dwelling place of him that is fallen. Unsere and Lilith. O rise from the abyss: the lower abyss underneath you, let them serve you! Govern those that govern: cast down such as fall! Bring forth with those that increase and destroy the rotten! No place let it remain in one number: add and diminish until the stars be numbered! Arise, move, and appear before the covenant of his mouth, which he has sworn unto us is his justice. Open the mysteries of your creation: and make us partakers of undefiled knowledge. Hail Satan! Hail Lucifer!

# Gematria and Magickal Tablets for Demonolatry

## Study Core

This lesson is meant to teach you the basics of how a tablet works. Tablets are an effective magickal tool because they are elementally, numerically, and alchemically balanced.

Let's just say that in most magickal traditions of the ceremonial variety, the complete knowledge for creating personalized tablets is something that's saved for the adepts of the upper echelon and inner circle. Most beginners start working with the basic Enochian tablets (watchtowers of the elementals).

You can also find some fascinating articles about enochian magick here including handy charts and how the numbers work out in various complex ways if you look on the Internet.

I can say from personal knowledge that many traditions make it deliberately confusing. In some traditions they even say that only males can create and use tablets. Obviously this myth came about from a time when women were denied certain knowledge and practices.

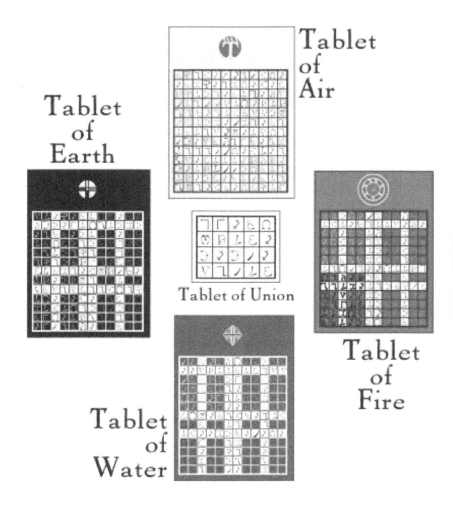

Tablet of Air

Tablet of Earth

Tablet of Union

Tablet of Fire

Tablet of Water

In the traditional Enochian Tablet (as with the watchtowers like on the previous page) you start with a square 13 down by 12 across (symbolic of the zodiac, alchemical properties, and aethers of the tree of life). The squares are broken down. The sixth and seventh squares in from the left side and 13 squares down and the seventh square down and 12 across represent the great cross (equal armed). Then you have the four quadrants, which are elemental as well as alchemical. The quadrants are 6 down and 5 across. Each quadrant is further broken down into kerubic squares, lesser squares, and the sephirothic cross (christian oriented obviously since the whole system of Enochian magick was originally Egyptian and converted to a Christian bent with angels et al)

But all of this will just confuse you because there are many ways to create magickal tablets that are elementally, alchemically, and numerically balanced and attuned to a certain deity (Daemonic or other).

I do think it's important that all students of Demonolatry learn as much as they possibly can about other schools of occult thought including Enochian tablets because it's all interconnected with Hermetics, which is the foundation for Demonolatry anyhow.

So instead of starting with Enochian outright, this is how my teacher taught me.

Once you start with the basics you can work your way forward and the Enochian system will make more sense. We started simple with basic Gematria and the English language. First, on a piece of paper write out the Demon's name you want to create the tablet for.

On the next pages you will find the values for letters (there are many other considerations depending on how complex you want your tablets to be) .

**Note** *just FYI - you should know that in Enochian tablets, each letter in english also corresponds to a zodiac sign and element as well as tarot card even before it's translated to the Enochian alphabet to give you an idea how complex this can get.*

Here are the Gematraic values for each letter in English (for letters with two values, the first is the primary value and the second is the secondary or alternate value):

A=6
B=5
C=300
D=4
E=10
F=3
G=8
H=1
I=60
J=60
K=300
L=8
M=90
N=50
O=30
P=9
Q=40
R=100
S=7
T=9, 3
U= 70
V= 70

W=70
X=400
Y=60
Z=9,3

First, let's start out by figuring out the gematria value of your name. Experiment with this using your name and the names of others to discover the hidden meaning in the numbers of a name. Use the Sepher Sephiroth or The Enochian Workbook for the meanings behind values of various numbers.

You can get meanings from the Sepher Sephiroth. Most people have a copy of *Crowley's 777 and Other Writings*. If you don't, I suggest getting one. It has the Sepher Sephiroth in it. Though you might want to stay away from the Hebraic Gematria at first because it can be confusing.

Let's do a tablet for Lucifer. It's a short name. First you want to figure out the value of Lucifer.

L = 8
U = 70
C= 300
I = 60
F= 3
E=10
R=100


Add all these numbers together. You get a grand total of 551.

You can further break down 551

5 + 5 + 1 = 11

Break 11 down further as $1 + 1 = 2$.

That is the lowest property you can reduce it to. 551 has no value, but 11 is a number that has the meaning, *"the special fire or light of the sacred magick of light/life"*. The number 2 is the Sephira of Wisdom. This obviously describes Lucifer very well.

Now you can kind of decide on the size of square you want and how you are going to choose to arrange it. Mind you this is not necessarily Enochian magick - it's simply a method of creating effective magickal tablets that will teach you about Gematria and all the alchemical and elemental properties of the mathematical construction of a tablet. These tablets, I've found, are just as effective as any.

Personally - I'd choose to create a 9x9 square only because I'd want the representation of the nine divinities and the ninth sephiroth represents the foundation or basis. The nine divinities are the foundation or basis of Demonolatry so this works.

This means you'll have a total of 81 squares to work with. Draw this up on a sheet of graph paper and use a highlighter to color the fifth row across and the fifth row down. Now you have an equal armed cross and four quadrants.

For now - let's stick with English. On the highlighted row down, skip the very first square. Now spell LUCIFER - one letter per square - going down. Do the same across. The I will be in the same place so they will intersect at the exact same point.

Right now let's say your top left quadrant is AIR (becase you want to start with the element of Lucifer). For whatever reason, let's assume your top right quadrant is WATER. The bottom left quadrant is EARTH, the bottom right quadrant is FIRE (for this example's purpose). There are four alchemical properties associated with certain combinations so you can place the elemental quadrants where you want them just in case you didn't want air at the top left.

Elemental Alchemical Properties:
- Air + Water = Humidity
- Earth + Fire = Dryness
- Earth + Water = Cold
- Fire + Air = Heat.

You could also break this down into zodiac decans but we won't go that far.

Now technically you could spell Lucifer diagonally through the quadrants as well, but let's not. Instead, Let's condense the elementals to four letters each. Lucifer is LCFR, Leviathan will become LVTN, Belial will become BELL, and Flereous will become FLRS.

With another highlighter or colored pencil of a different color (you can use colors of the elements if you wish) in each quadrant color the four center squares of each quadrant. From right to left, top to bottom, spell out the four letters of each Demon name.

**EXERCISE** - what is the numeric (gematraic) value of each of the elementals spelt as they are? What is the lowest value you can take that number down to? How many empty squares do you have left over? The answers are on the next page.

| | | | | | | | | | |
|---|---|---|---|---|---|---|---|---|---|
| | L | C | | L | | L | V | |
| | F | R | | U | | T | N | |
| | | | | C | | | | |
| | L | U | C | I | F | E | R | |
| | | | | F | | | | |
| | B | E | | E | | F | L | |
| | L | L | | R | | R | S | |
| | | | | | | | | |

30 Squares Used
81 Squares Total
51 Squares Left Over

LCFR = 411 to 6
LVTN = 92 to 11 to 2
BELL = 31 to 4
FLRS = 118 to 10 or to 1

# READING TWO

So now you know the basic construction of a tablet we are going to work on building a tablet more complex.

How about adding a sigil to a tablet? Aside from a pictorial representation (actual sigil) added to a tablet somewhere at its midpoint, why not build one right into it?

Get a piece of graph paper.

Let's start with another 9x9 tablet because it's small and easy to work with. Plus, 9 + 9 = 18 and 1 + 8 = 9. You may choose a larger tablet with a different numeric meaning.

For the purpose of this example - we will work with the following sigil (Verrine):

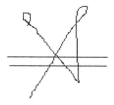

Since I want the value of the sigil to be 1 because it represents the Sephiroth Kether in the tree of life. (You can choose any value for the sigil you want) Were I using Crowley's Enochian – 1 would be representative of the letter A. In the modernized Enochian number system we're using for the purpose of this course of study (see reading one) the letter H is the only letter with the value of 1. Therefore we will use the letter H.

| H |   |   |   |   |   |   |   | H |
|---|---|---|---|---|---|---|---|---|
|   | H |   |   |   |   |   | H |   |
|   |   | H |   |   |   | H | H |   |
|   |   |   | H |   | H |   | H |   |
| H | H | H | H | H | H | H | H | H |
| H | H | H | H | H | H | H | H | H |
|   |   | H |   |   |   | H | H |   |
|   | H |   |   |   |   |   | H |   |
| H |   |   |   |   |   |   |   |   |

Can you see the likeness of the sigil within the tablet? You can color the tablet any way you wish. I chose blue for this particular tablet because blue represents healing to me. It also represents relaxation and renewal. Choose colors that represent the sigil and tablet purpose most closely.

How many squares does this sigil use? How many squares are left over?

Squares used – 34
Squares left over – 47

An alternative to creating a Verrine based tablet would be:

| | V | E | R | R | I | N | E | |
|---|---|---|---|---|---|---|---|---|
| V | | | | | | | | E |
| E | | | | | | | | N |
| R | | | | | | | | I |
| R | | | | | | | | R |
| I | | | | | | | | R |
| N | | | | | | | | E |
| E | | | | | | | | V |
| | E | N | I | R | R | E | V | |

In this instance, the actual sigil of Verrine sits at the center of the tablet and his name encircles the tablet on all four sides. There is still enough room for elemental quadrants here, and numerous other properties based on the purpose of the tablet.

How many squares does this sigil use? How many are left over?

- Squares used - 29
- Squares left over – 52

You might wonder why I keep asking you how many squares are used and how many are left over. The reason for this is that you will need to know what is left over to eventually complete the tablet.

You can also create the tablet first, then embellish it with the sigils wanted surrounding it.

Remember, the tablets in these examples are not completed. That is a surprise for the next lesson. In the meantime, let's discuss, more in depth, more aspects of the magickal tablet. Not only can individual quadrants or words within the tablet be added up for numeric significance, but they can be added across and down and as a whole for their numeric value.

A simple example to illustrate this would be:

| H | H | H | H | H | H | H | H | H | = 9 |
|---|---|---|---|---|---|---|---|---|-----|
| H | H | H | H | H | H | H | H | H | = 9 |
| H | H | H | H | H | H | H | H | H | = 9 |
| H | H | H | H | H | H | H | H | H | = 9 |
| H | H | H | H | H | H | H | H | H | = 9 |
| H | H | H | H | H | H | H | H | H | = 9 |
| H | H | H | H | H | H | H | H | H | = 9 |
| H | H | H | H | H | H | H | H | H | = 9 |
| H | H | H | H | H | H | H | H | H | = 9 |
| = 9 | = 9 | = 9 | = 9 | = 9 | = 9 | = 9 | = 9 | = 9 | = 81 |

The value of the columns and rows of this generic tablet = 81
$8 + 1 = 9$

Or $81 + 81 = 162$

$1 + 6 + 2 = 9$

Now let's try a more complex example (you might want to copy this page to calculate it):

| L | S | A | T | A | N | A | S | N | = |
|---|---|---|---|---|---|---|---|---|---|
| E | L | B | A | L | A | B | L | A | = |
| V | H | U | L | U | L | U | H | H | = |
| I | H | P | C | C | C | P | H | T | = |
| A | L | U | C | I | F | E | R | A | = |
| T | H | P | F | F | F | P | H | I | = |
| H | H | E | L | E | L | E | H | V | = |
| A | R | B | A | R | A | B | R | E | = |
| N | S | A | N | A | T | A | S | L | = |
| = | = | = | = | = | = | = | = | = |  |

I've left space in the table for you to total all of the values of each row and column. Once you get the values down and across – add the value of the column and row together and then take it down to its lowest calculation.

# Reading Three

## Tablet Properties

### Colors:

Here are some basic color correspondences you can work with. If any of these aspects doesn't seem to fit for you – you are more than welcome to add colors that you associate to the purpose of your tablet more readily.

- **Red and Orange** – Fire, action, love, lust relationships, creative work, anger, passion.
- **Blue and Gray** – Water, emotions, empathy, intuition, creative process, healing, divination, fertility.
- **Yellow and White** – Air, enlightenment, education, life lessons, planning.
- **Brown, Black, Green** – Earth, stability, financial matters, mundane matters, physical aspects of fertility, knowledge, trust, grounding/balancing.

### Numbers special to you:
Consider numbers that might be special to you like birthdates, anniversaries, etc...

### Alchemical and Elemental:

- **Elemental** = a part of the natural universe essential to life. Earth, air, fire, water.
- **Alchemical** = parts of the natural universe combined to create something different. Humidity, dryness, cold, and heat are some examples.

**Demonic Properties:**

See the various Demon listings in this book to find Demons that correspond to your tablet's purpose.

**Planetary Properties:**

Ruling Planets

Sun This is the center of existence. In astrology it symbolizes everything we are trying to become, the center around which all our activity in life revolve. This Planet (also known as a luminary and a star) represents the self, one's personality and ego, the spirit and what it is that makes the individual unique. It rules the zodiacal sign Leo, a fire sign. Everything in the horoscope ultimately revolves around this singular body. It is the Sun which gives strength to the other Planets, which is why this Planet occupies a key role in Astrology. It is the symbol of strength, vigor, wisdom, dignity, ardor and generosity, and the ability for a person to function as a mature individual.

Moon Since the Moon is closest to Earth it influences us more deeply than any other Planet. The effect is very personal, very intimate. Whereas the Sun gives us our spirit, it's the Moon which gives us our soul. The Moon is goddess-like in that it symbolizes mother and the relationship between woman and child. The moon (also known as a luminary) speaks to the women in one's life and their role as nurturer. This planet rules zodiacal sign Cancer one among the watery signs.

This Planet implores us to express ourselves clearly. Mercury represents your capacity to understand the desires of your own will and to translate those desires into action. In other words it is the planet of mind and the power of communication. Through mercury we develop an ability to think, write, speak and observe- to be aware of world around us. When Mercury goes retrograde (the appearance of traveling backward) our communications will be challenged. Mercury rules the zodiacal sign Gemini and Virgo.

Mercury

It symbolizes the harmony and radiance of a rare and elusive quality, the beauty itself. Venus is all about pleasure, especially pleasure shared with someone else. This Planet concerns itself with love, romance and harmony in our emotional attachments, marriages, friendships and other unions (like business partnerships). Venus also deals with the pleasure we derive from our possessions. Luxuries (jewelry, paintings, expensive cars), a beautiful home and a sense of refinement all belong to Venus's interests. This Planet ruling the zodiacal signs Taurus and Libra appreciates the exquisite nature of things.

Venus

Mars is the action Planet of the Zodiac. Your Mars Sign defines what you desire and how you express that desire. This Planet commands you to stand up, be noticed and get things done etc. Ambition and competition are also within Mars's realm. Mars also rule the power and confident expression of the individual. Mars is the ruling planet of zodiacal signs Scorpio and Aries.

Mars

Jupiter influence thinking capacity of a person. In astrology it rules good luck and good cheer, health, wealth, optimism, happiness, success and

Jupiter joy. It is a symbol of opportunity and always opens way for new opportunities in life. Jupiter is the minimization of limitation and the emphasis on spirituality and potential. While our success, accomplishments and prosperity are all within Jupiter's realm, its negative influence can deteriorate into laziness and sloth. It rules the zodiacal signs Sagittarius and Pices belonging to fire and watery elements respectively.

Saturn plays the role of a taskmaster in the Zodiac. Saturn commands us to get to work and to work hard. Saturn rules time, old age and sobriety.

Saturn It can bring depression, gloom, jealousy and greed, or serious acceptance of responsibilities out of which success will develop. Learning life's lessons is key to this Planet, in keeping with its role as teacher. It rules the earth sign Capricorn and the air sign Aquarius.

Uranus brings with it a new way of looking at things, and its approach is best met with an expanded consciousness. Uranus rules unexpected

Uranus change, upheaval, revolution. It is the symbol of total independence and asserts the freedom of an individual from all restriction and restraint. It is a breakthrough planet and indicates talent, originality and genius in a horoscope. This planet rules Aquarius an air sign.

Neptune ruling the watery sign Pisces, awakens a sense of higher responsibility often causing guilt, worry, anxieties or delusions. In short, Neptune is

Neptune creating an illusion -- of what is enchanting on the outside and captivating within. Sleep and dreams are also lorded over by this Planet.

Pluto This Planet influence transformation, regeneration and rebirth. This Planet is about all that is secret and undercover, that which is hidden from view. Pluto starts its influence with a minor event or insignificant incident that might even go unnoticed. Pluto rules the fire sign Aries and water sign Scorpio.

Letters and The Zodiac and Alphabet (from Modern Enochian Magick examples):

A = Taurus
B = Aries
C, K = Fire
D = Spirit
E = Virgo
F = Cauda
G = Cancer
H = Air
I, J, Y = Sagittarius
L = Cancer
M = Aquarius
N = Scorpio
O = Libra
P = Leo
Q = Water
R = Pisces
S = Gemini
T = Leo
U,V,W = Capricorn
X = Earth

$Z = Leo$

# Reading Four

## Completing the Tablets

In reading one we started with the following tablet.

| | | | | | | | | | |
|---|---|---|---|---|---|---|---|---|---|
| | L | C | | L | | L | V | |
| | F | R | | U | | T | N | |
| | | | | C | | | | |
| | L | U | C | I | F | E | R | |
| | | | | F | | | | |
| | B | E | | E | | F | L | |
| | L | L | | R | | R | S | |
| | | | | | | | | | |

Now I am going to complete this tablet. This is an Air Tablet. It already has all of the Elementals present except for Satan. I am going to include Lucifuge Rofocale, too. Since Lucifuge Rofocale fits balanced around the outer edge (and represents Daath) that is where I will place him. Satan will wrap around each element in an L shape. In this instance I used both gray and yellow for air, blue for water, bluish green for earth, and red for fire. I used a deeper gold for Lucifuge Rofocale to show his fire side. I chose a deep gray for Satan to represent the whole and the balance within.

| L | E | L | A | C | O | F | O | R |
|---|---|---|---|---|---|---|---|---|
| U | L | C | S | L | S | L | V | E |
| C | F | R | A | U | A | T | N | G |
| I | N | A | T | C | T | A | N | U |
| F | L | U | C | I | F | E | R | F |
| U | S | A | T | F | T | A | S | I |
| G | B | E | A | E | A | F | L | C |
| E | L | L | N | R | N | R | S | U |
| R | O | F | O | C | A | L | E | L |

This table contains the following Numeric Properties (you get to figure it out):

Vertical Value:
Horizontal Value:
Total Value:

This tablet's sole purpose is a representation of the air elemental. Does the calculation prove true to its purpose?

When I translate the tablet to Enochian, it looks like this:

Your assignment for this reading is to complete one of the following tablets based on YOUR personal preference. If you choose the Tablet of Lucifer from Lesson 1, modify it differently from the one above. (See end of lesson to learn how to do this in word)

**EXERCISE: Choose one of the following tablets and complete it.**

| | | | | | | | | | |
|---|---|---|---|---|---|---|---|---|---|
| | L | C | | L | | L | V | | |
| | F | R | | U | | T | N | | |
| | | | | C | | | | | |
| | L | U | C | I | F | E | R | | |
| | | | | F | | | | | |
| | B | E | | E | | F | L | | |
| | L | L | | R | | R | S | | |
| | | | | | | | | | |

319

# Tablets Questions and Answers

This section is included, with answers, to see if you have fully understood the tablet readings. Work through them slowly. If you don't get the same answer, try to figure out why.

## PART 1

**1. What is the value of your name and its meaning according to the Sepher Sephiroth?**

**2. Calculate the value of LEVIATHAN. What do you get? What is the lowest number value you can get from it? What are the meanings of Leviathan based on these numbers and the Sepher Sephiroth? Based on the Sephir Sephiroth (Crowley) and LVTN.**

LVTN= 486. =(18)=(9). (18) Hatred, the antique serpent. (9)= Fire of Sorcery, Beloved, enchanter, and Chesed. (486)= foundations (as in LVTN's place around sephira)

**or – based on Gematraic numeric system presented (using primary number):**  2

Leviathan= 220 2+2+0=4

220: The elect, heroina, augusta, domina, ye shall cleave, cean, elegant, giants

4: father, hollow, a vein, proud.

Using the secondary value: 214 = 7 – the lord of armies, the Sephira of firmness and victory.

320

**3. The numbers 7, 6, 9/3, 6, 50 spells what name in English? What is the value of this name and it's meanings according to the Sepher Sephiroth?**

Satan. Primary: (78)=(15)=(6). Steam/Vapor, Pride, # Geburah , Monogram for the eternal, He who impels. Secondary: 72 = 9

**4. Why do some letters have more than one number associated with them? (A basic answer is fine, but feel free to write more if you've done in depth research into this.)**

The primary and secondary have to do with placement value. For example the primary would be used in cases of capitals indicative of proper nouns denoting the specific vs. the common. The primary and the secondary. The first number is primary, and the second number is secondary. Use the secondary number if the letter is in the middle of a name.

**5. Why was a 9 x9 square chosen for the tablet of Lucifer created in the reading example?**

Because the 9th Sephiroth, Yesod, represents the foundation, and the foundation of Demonolatry are the nine divinities.

# PART 2

**Assignment Tablet**

**1. What is the total calculation of the assignment tablet in reading two (using the gematria letter number values from reading one)? Did you use a primary or secondary value for T? Notice anything about the vertical and horizontal calculation using the primary vs. secondary values? Either way - the total value of the tablet still comes out the same when condensed to the lowest number. What is its lowest calculation?**

Total calculation Primary = 5520 = 12 = 3
              Non Primary = 5484 = 21 = 3
3 = The Sephira of understanding.
Down and Across the non primary values are both
2742 = 15 = 6

**2. Explain why I might have chosen the colors I chose. Would you have chosen differently - and why?**

- Blue – Leviathan – Water (element)
- Red – Satanas – (Fire) the whole.
- Yellow – Lucifer – Air (element)
- Green – BAL = 19 = 10 = 1 – The whole. Green was chosen to balance the tablet, which was lacking in earth and stability.
- Gray – H – has value of 1 – the whole – the Sephira of Satan – Gray seemed an appropriate color due to the subtle shades of gray in everything.
- Light Blue – P – has the value of 9 – the whole. Light blue, for me, is a calming/balancing color and 9 is the foundation or balance.

**3. Why, do you think, I used 8 H's and 4 P's. Look at numeric values and colors to figure it out.**

H = 1 and there are 8 polarities in the nine divinities.
P = 9 and 9 x 4 = 36 = 9

**4. What is BAL? Why, do you suppose I chose it?**

BAL = 19 and represents manifestation and contains a balance of light and darkness. Further broken down it is 10, which is the Sephira of Kingdom, exalted. Further broken down to 1 – it is the whole. BAL (a shortened version of Baal – the primary Earth) connects the physical to all that is, and is representative of the missing earth in this tablet to achieve balance.

**5. What does all of this information suggest about the purpose of this tablet?**

This is a tablet for balance, to achieve a connection with all that is. It would be used in ascension, for divination, and/or for Ordainment of members of the Priesthood. It represents an understanding of the whole and the connection between the mundane and the spiritual.

**SIGIL TABLETS READING**

**1. Can you figure out why I spelt Verrine forward and backward around the outer edges of the second reading tablet?**

For balance in the tablet top and bottom.
- V's in opposite corners for balance = 140 = 5
- E's in opposite corners for balance = 20 = 2

**2. What would be the numeric meaning of a tablet 48 x 48?**

2304 = 9 -- the same as a 9x9 tablet.

**3. How can someone choose colors for certain aspects of a tablet?**

Based on elemental, purposeful, alchemical, and/or planetary correspondences that have meaning to the Demonolator him or herself.

# READING THREE

**1.Calculate the Value of the Tablet in Reading 3:**
    Vertical value: 3870
    Horizontal value: 4113
    Total value: 7983  7+9+8+3= 27  2+7=9

**What is the tablet that I created in the final reading for?**

The foundation of Air

# Modified Middle Pillar Ritual

The Middle Pillar Ritual (MPR) is perfectly compatible with Demonolatry because Demonolatry is also Hermetic. I'll do the MPR after an elemental balancing if I've been feeling tired. The energy it provides usually lasts about a week before it has to be repeated. Or I'll do it before a rite where I expend a lot of energy. I simply change the words from the traditional MPR. See the Chakra chart in the Astral Projection section of the book.

The elemental balancing is really the closest I can think of an actual "Demonolatry" ritual that will increase personal energy. So consider both of these when you feel depleted. Do this inside an elemental circle for best results.

1. Stand in your Temple (or other location) Arms are stretched out straight to both sides. On your right is the Black Pillar of Severity; on your left is the White Pillar of Mercy. You stand in between as the Middle Pillar of Balance.

2. A blindingly brilliant white light, the Light of Satan (Ain Soph Aur is fine as well) originates far above your head, coming from the Crown. (Saharshra).

3. The light descends to the top of your forehead, forming a sphere the size of your head. Vibrate, strongly: EH-EI-EH ("I AM")

4. When this is felt strongly, allow the light to descend to the Daath center (throat chakkra).) Vibrate: OM (or perhaps even the enn of Lucifuge Rofocal since I think we decided he is likely Daath)

5. Allow the Light to descend further to the heart center (Tiphareth/Anahatta chakra). Vibrate the Enn of Belial.

6. Allow the Light to descend through the Solar Plexus, down to the Svadisthana Chakra (generational center) at Yesod. Vibrate the Enn of Flereous.

7. Allow the Light to descend further, through the Muladhara Chakra (root center) and all the way down to the earth, gaining density as it progresses. Vibrate your personal words of power. (See Demonolatry Lesson Core)

8. The light surrounds you.

9. Allow it to ascend back up to center in the Heart, where it becomes established in fullness.

10. From this Center the Light may be channeled as a healing energy, or aimed at an object. The Light may also be established in the Heart and utilized as a catalyst for meditative states and visions.

# The Great Work

The Great Work is, essentially, the journey of the discovery of the Self and the individual's place in the universe as well as his relationship with the Demonic Divine.

This section is provided for Adepts who find themselves at a stalemate for where to go next on their path. There is no prescribed study for adepts. No outline for them to follow. It becomes, at that point, your responsibility to do the things that will help you move forward on your journey. On the following pages you'll find topics of interest, books to look into, and some exercises worthy of your contemplation.

## Alchemy and the Philosopher's Stone

A friend and I were talking one day about what occult symbols could be used as a pictorial representation of the Philosopher's stone. We discussed the pentagram both rightside up and inverse, we discussed the tree of life, and many other symbols. I finally decided we could apply the principles of the philospher's stone to the Ankh. Here is what I told him, below.

*The Ankh represents 3 because it has 3 points (the physical body, the psychological body, and the spiritual body), making a triangle (on top of the elements). Obviously it is the physical and psychological that conceive the spiritual. It also looks somewhat human in shape to represent man. It's activating quality is its inherent balance and attunement to the human animal. The "eye" of the ankh sees into the window of the soul. Let's take a look at an ankh for a moment. I labeled it.* **See the following page.**

In addition, I could have likely gone further and explored the trinity of the Nine Divinities and the Demonic aspects present within the Ankh. I would like to ask the adept to contemplate the image of the ankh on the next page and see if you can define it using the Nine Divinities. There is a triad, the five elements... only the ninth is hidden. Can you find it? I would place the ninth in the center of the triangle. Two Demons reside at the point of fire. Which ones? These are the questions you should ask yourself of your symbol while doing the following exercise.

**Adept Exercise:** Can you think of any religious or occult symbols that could adequately be a pictorial representation of the Philosophers Stone? Do as we did and draw the symbol. Then label it and explain why.

In addition**, read the following books**:
- The Philospher's Stone by Israel Regardie
- The Hermetic Arcanum

- The Chemical Marriage
- The Chymical Wedding

You might be able to find these books online in PDF.

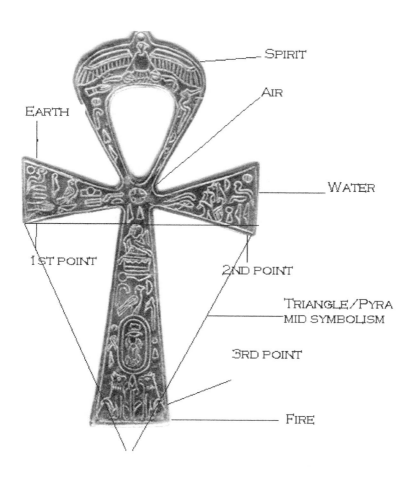

# Pathworking

Pathworking is a long and difficult process meant to expand the mind, deepen spiritual awareness, find our unique place as part of the whole, and to harness the innate wisdom and strength of our Selves so we can live the most fulfilling life possible in the here and now.

Many times upon our paths we stumble or find ourselves distracted by the pretty flowers on the side of the road, creating a stalemate. That's when most people either switch religions or keep searching for that one thing that will make their lives fulfilling and meaningful. So we look to books. While books can offer advice and increase our knowledge and understanding, true understanding comes from experience. It comes from communing with Demons and it comes from within.

This means that instead of just reading about the rituals of any particular tradition, perhaps we should participate (through comfortable modification to make sure the Demons are respected and acknowledged) and get our hands dirty to some extent. We need to explore different things. This goes beyond strictly spiritual related material. Going out into the world and trying new things can be spiritually gratifying and give our lives meaning and purpose. We can put these experiences into a spiritual context and later reflect on the experience to learn how much it really meant to us.

So in discussing path work, we're also discussing the experiences of life and how those things, even though not always spiritual, can affect our spiritual well being. For example, I once knew a woman who loved to read about traveling abroad. But she had never been. She could tell you all about The Tower of London, historically speaking, but had never experienced being there for herself. So one year she finally went. When she got back and told the story of what she had seen, you could see a sparkle in her eye and the awe and reverence she had for the experience. She later admitted that the experience itself had been mentally, emotionally, and spiritually gratifying.

So when you find yourself stuck in your pathwork and you find yourself bored with the same rituals, prayers, and spiritual workings you've been doing for years, consider another approach to pull you from your stalemate.

- Do something you've never done before.
- Read up on a magickal practice or religious tradition you've never explored.
- Take classes in something you've always wanted to learn.
- Take a trip to a foreign country or go someplace you've never been.
- Go out with your friends for a night on the town.
- Stay home and watch a movie you've never seen.
- Learn a new language.

Basically – live! Life itself is the most spiritual experience of all. It cannot be found in a ritual or book, or in a prayer. Experience itself is its own reward and life has many lessons and secrets to teach you.

## Relationships with Demons

Many practitioners, after years of work, may find themselves disconnected from the Demons, or wishing to strengthen the existing bonds they've built. In my experience of many years as a Demonolatress, I've discovered that we often become complacent and take for granted that which already exists.

After time, we miss that rush we get when we invoke a Demon into a ritual circle. We miss the excitement of the first time we developed a bond with a particular Demon.

Never will you notice your complacency more than when the Demonic energy you've built up over the years just isn't there anymore. This happened to me. I had invited a ceremonial magician (unbeknownst to me) into my home and he commenced commanding the Demons in my home. Consequently, they all left. That's often what pissed off Demons do.

Yes, you heard me. The Demons were so offended (as was I), they left despite the fact that it wasn't me who had done it. Absent of Demonic energy, my home felt empty, unwelcoming, and suddenly I was a guest in my own house.

I ended up having to do a series of rites inviting the Demons back into my home until it felt right again. It was at that point that I realized just how much I took my relationship with the Demons for granted. They had been there for so long, I had forgotten what it was like to not have the Demonic energy ever-present around me.

This may be the case with the Demonolator who is seeking a new relationship with a Demon, or who misses the excitement of their early days when everything was so new and there were so many secrets to uncover. I'm not sure what the answer is to help renew the newness. You cultivate your relationship with the Demons each time you pray, or perform a rite, or do a magickal working. Each offering, each sigil, and each incense or oleum you make strengthens that bond. Every meditation and ascension brings you closer to the Demonic energies.

But much like marriage, the newness wears off and it does become old hat. Now I don't suggest commanding Demons or inviting those who do into your home just so you can realize you have taken the Demons for granted. What you can do, however, is develop a series of rites to reintroduce yourself to the Demons you wish to renew contact with. Seek Them during ascension to see if They have suggestions on ways to renew your excitement and discovery of Them. Be creative and find ways to cultivate that relationship.

If you've never tried a mental relationship (sexual or other) with a particular Demon, perhaps you should try that. It's up to you to rediscover and kindle that relationship. Also, consider working with Demons you've never worked with before even if they aren't a part of your preferred pantheon. There are thousands to choose from and there are many ways to explore Demons, commune with them, and honor them. Basically, you have to get creative and pull yourself out of the stalemate. With this experience you will grow spiritually and continue to cultivate life long relationships with numerous aspects of the Demonic Divine.

# The Solitary Demonolator
# &
# The Adept

The road to enlightenment leads to the Self. This can make the practice of any spiritual path a lonely one. Many people want instant enlightenment. They want to find that one book or path that will quickly give them what they want. Or they seem to think belonging to a group will get them from A to Z more expeditiously. True, books and groups can help one through the basics faster. On the flipside, the faster you learn, retain, and put into use the basics, the sooner you may find yourself at a stalemate. What comes next can't be "taught". You either get it or you don't.

What most people don't realize is that their spirituality and connection with the Demons and Satan relies on them. Their growth through adepthood depends on the individual and the Self Work the individual does. That may sound easy, but it isn't. The Great Work of getting to "know thyself" is a life long journey laden with set-backs, disaster, confusion, loss of faith, profound disappointment, and many other hard lessons. The rewards, however, far outweigh those obstacles.

Once you get past the basics, the newness will wear off. You might feel like you're at a stalemate doing the same things over and over again. You might feel that you want something new to learn – some hidden secret to uncover. Unfortunately, this is where the intense Self Work begins. Belonging to a group or reading a book cannot replace the Self Work and no one can really tell you how to proceed. So, for all intents and purposes, at this point we all become solitary on our individual paths to universal consciousness, enlightenment, and self-empowerment. Books like this one exist to merely help one along one's path. Your experiences, while they might be similar to some else's, will always be unique to you.

For the Solitary Demonolator, it can be frustrating doing this work alone. The positive side to this is you become more self-reliant and independent. You are forced to use your intuition. With a group, some Demonolators may come to rely on the teacher too much, and will ignore their intuition. They are dependent and often have to be *weaned*. So there are pros and cons to both groups and working solitary.

For the Solitary Practitioner, this book should be guiding you through the basics of respectful Demon worship and regular practice. For the Adept, this book has hopefully given you some material to chew on and perhaps a different perspective.

**For the Solitary Practitioners, work on the following:**

- Learning about and working with the Demons.
- Understanding the basic fundamentals of Demonolatry, spiritual alchemy, and the Hermetic.
- Understanding (through practicing) prayer, offerings, and ritual.
- Learning the basics of Demonolatry Magick (The Art of Creative Magick will be very helpful if you wish to continue your studies there).

**For the Adept, work on the following:**

- Contemplate the Philosophers Stone and consider all occult symbols in relation to it.
- Consider The Great Work and devise a plan of study and practice to get you to where you want to be on your spiritual path.
- Write your own rituals and perform them.
- Practice ascension and see what wisdom the Demons have to offer.
- Continue to broaden your life experience base and try new things.

# Sex Magick

I think it's very important for us to address the topic of Sex Magick. Sex magick is perfectly acceptable and appropriate for Demonolatry Rites as long as all participants are of legal age and willing. **Practice safe sex always!** For those solitary practitioners who might be teenagers, masturbation is perfectly acceptable and normal and don't let anyone tell you otherwise.

The basic premise behind sex magick is during the middle of the rite, after the purpose of the rite has been clearly defined, the individual or persons involved masturbate or have intercourse. During climax, all persons involved must shift their attention to the purpose of the Rite, thus sending the energy of climax to serve that purpose.

Some rites call for the individual to lay down upon or sit upon the sigil of the Demon being invoked, and masterbate on it, using sexual fluid to anoint the sigil before burning it.

337

There are many different types of Sex Magick based rites out there. In some instances they may be group related, couples, or individuals. They may involve intercourse or just masturbation, and sexual secretions may or may not be collected for use in making oleums, or anointing the participants of the ritual.

In some of the older rites, which I do not include here because I do not have permission to share them, one group member might be chosen to be masturbated (by someone else) in front of the entire sect, or a select few, or one other person for the purpose of collecting sexual fluid for special oleums. (Obviously with this person's consent.)

Others have used Sex Magick as a way to symbolically act out sexual relationships with Daemons. I have had a good number of people approach me over the years wanting to discuss the possibility of having sexual intercourse with Demons as many people seem to think there is a rite you can do to make such a thing happen. How do we know that sex is also a Demon need? It may be a human one, but we would be foolish and arrogant to assume that Demons have the same needs as us. We can barely comprehend their nature and existence, let alone their sexual needs – if any.

Sexual relationships with Demons can take place imaginatively (i.e. fantasy), and emotionally. These self-created psychological "relationships" can cause physical reactions such as erection, lubrication, muscle contraction, phantom sensations of penetration, and orgasm. So it can be physical in this particular sense. But it's still one-sided on this plane of existence and takes place largely within our own minds. A self created experience we call it.

I am not trying to dismiss the personal experiences of anyone reading this who might claim to have a genuine physical sexual relationship with a Daemon, but the evidence of these alleged physical relationships is questionable and points to the psychological rather than the physical. Most serious, adept Demonolators admit having sexual fantasies and sexual dreams involving Demons. However, I have never met an adept who believes in a physical skin-on-skin sexual relationship with Demons. They've never had it happen to them. So the question then arises, "Wouldn't Demons, if they're going to sleep with Humans, start with the Humans they already have relationships with? Especially if the Demon was invited freely by a highly attractive and desirable Demonolator or Demonolatress?"

You would think the answer to that would be yes. But despite how much we try, the closest Demonolators can get to sex with Demons is fantasy that fulfils the needs of our Selves. On the positive side, these types of relationships can emotionally solidify a bond between a Demonolator and a Demon, and can be used as offerings and positive energy transference to a particular Demon. They can also be satisfying in the absence of a real human partner. It is my belief that anyone claiming to sleep with Demons has a rich and fulfilling fantasy life, and that's nothing to be ashamed of. However, I also believe that we should be honest with our Selves and others and admit that we have psychological and emotional bonds with Demons – not necessarily "physical" Demon lovers, regardless how real the experiences our minds give us may seem.

# Blood Rites & Sacrifice

## Blood Rites

Blood Rites are defined as rites wherein blood is an integral part of the offering. It is suggested that you have a diabetic pen and lancets available to draw blood for ritual as necessary. Blood, including menstrual blood, has been used to anoint candles, people, added to inks, wines, and oleums. Blood from the Self, taken in the *least destructive manner possible and* used during a Blood Rite is considered, by many Demonolators to be the highest and most sacred form of sacrifice to a Demon.

Back before we knew so much about blood born diseases, many Demonolators used daggers to their palms to draw blood with little concern for infection.

Blood (a few drops) from each member of a group was often placed in a chalice of wine from which the entire sect drank. Nowadays, with what we now know about AIDS and Hepatitis and other blood born disease, this practice is not safe and has been abandoned by many. It is sometimes still practiced between close friends, and more often between married couples who swap bodily fluids anyway. Regardless what you choose to do, always consider your safety and the safety of others. Do not practice blood magick wherin blood is shared in drink with those who you don't know well (i.e. know their medical history).

## Sacrifices

I have stated elsewhere in this book that Demonolators do not practice sacrifice of non-food animals, or other people because the Demons do not demand such things. To Sacrifice means to make sacred. The most sacred sacrifice of all is a few drops of blood from your Self. Sexual fluids or tears can compensate for Blood Sacrifice if you're squeamish.

Some people claim that blood sacrifice is necessary to produce the right amount of energy for magickal work. In this, they are suggesting that perhaps Demonic magick is not as effective if a blood sacrifice is not performed. I vehemently disagree. I know that the Demonic magickal workings of myself and other Demonolators are exremely potent and effective despite the fact that none of us have ever performed a ritual blood sacrifice of an animal.

If what these people say is indeed, true - then people like us probably ought not practice ritual sacrifice anyway. I know that I already find myself surprised (and sometimes unsettled) at how effective my magickal work is and how quickly it manifests the desired change without blood sacrifice of another living creature. I shudder to think what would happen if this claim were true and Demonolators who were already working effective magick started performing blood sacrifice just to increase the energy produced. But I highly doubt the validity of this claim.

Curses can be and are an acceptable form of "sacrifice" as long as the person being cursed is deserving of it. Deserving means they have killed someone, raped someone, or destroyed another person's life in a way where the person was destroyed mentally, physically, or spiritually. Those are justifiable reasons for cursing.

Cursing Jane because she slept with Bob, and you like Bob and don't like Jane – well, that's just petty and likely a waste of energy and time. Your best bet there would be to curse the negative feelings you have toward the situation to get rid of that negativity rather than curse the person whose actions caused you to react so negatively. After all, Jane may not have known you liked Bob, or even if she did, she's not responsible for your reaction. You choose your reaction to people's actions. Every action causes and equal and/or opposite reaction. Plus, the Demons might give you a smack for doing something so petty. Keep that in mind.

*A word about curses (Again):* Do not feel guilt or regret for doing a curse or you only hurt yourself. Make sure it is just and you have considered it carefully. Wait three days before acting to make sure you aren't acting based on irrational thoughts and feelings. These are the basic laws all Demonolators should follow. Cursing should never be taken lightly. If you want to know more about cursing and why it can be a bad thing, check out Ellen Purswell's Goetic Demonolatry wherein she explains why some people can't be cursed or even healed through magickal work. Remember in the courtesies where it says we all have natural gifts bestowed upon us by Satan? Some people are naturally resistant to external energy unless it's invited. You could curse that person and that person could send your negativity back to you. And you may not have the natural ability to shield yourself from it. You might be an absorber. So before working Demonic magick on another person, even a deserving person, always take the time to consider this and figure it into your plan.

# Vi Baoith Raimi Kairty
# & The Demonic Name

## Vi Boith Raimi Kairty

Vi Boith Raimi Kairty is a personal sigil of power given to a practitioner not from the Matron/Patron Demon, but rather one of the Nine Divinities. This usually happens during ritual. The symbol may appear on a piece of parchment or may appear drawn on the altar. In several instances, it has been reported it appeared on the practitioner himself, only to later disappear. If you suspect you have been given Vi Boath Raimey Kairty, be sure to draw the symbol in your notebook or journal and keep it. This is your personal symbol of power and can be used during rites and Demonic magick to amplify your existing strengths and energy. Most Demonolators do not receive Vi Boath Raimey Kairty right away. It usually comes unexpectedly after a few years of dedicated practice and worship. We're not sure why this is the general rule, but I suspect it has something to do with the Demons giving these things wisely to people who will not abuse, and who are ready for, what they're given.

You can share your Vi Boath Raimey Kairty with someone else if you chose to, but it will be useless to another person. Nope – you can't even use someone else's against them, so don't even consider it. It is unique to you. Like a fingerprint, yes, but it has built in protections. If your energy isn't attached to it – it's rendered useless. Simple as that. I know this because we did an experiment where three of us shared our VBRKs. The rituals produced no results in all instances. But when you put the right VBRK with the right energy combination – the results of the rituals were stellar.

**The Demonic Name**

The Demonic Name is the name the Demons traditionally give an adept via a divination session done prior to the passage to adepthood rite. The use of the birth name at the beginning of the rite and Demonic name at the end of the rite is symbolic of the passage. For all Rites after adepthood the worshiper's Demonic name is used. For all Rites before adepthood, the worshiper's birth name is used.

However, in the absence of a group as in the case of many solitary practitioners, the Demons will often give you this name themselves. You might hear it over and over again in a dream, or find yourself drawn to the name. There are numerous methods Demons have used to give these names to Demonolators. Sometimes the names are odd. In other cases they seem quite normal. Contrary to belief, your Demonic Name cannot be used against you either (by someone who wishes to do you harm). So don't worry. It's simply the name the Demons know you by.

# Necromancy

You might be wondering why there is a very short chapter titled Necromancy in this book. What does Necromancy have to do with Demonolatry? Necromancy is basically communing with death in some form or another. Whether it be using divination practices to speak to the dead, aligning yourself with the death energy (raising the dead), honoring the dead, or coming to terms with death.

There is a whole school of Demonolatry thought and practice dedicated to the death Demons. See the Rite to Eurynomous, Ba(a)lberith, and Babaa(e)l to find information about the traditional ancestral altar and ways of honoring the dead. In addition to Rites honoring the Demons of Death, there are also numerous Rites to Eurynomous (and others) to align persons with the death energy, and to come to terms with death-like changes, or even death itself. An entire book discussing Demonolatry based Necromancy is forthcoming in 2007 (if not already out by the time you read this). It's a complex topic worthy of its own book and I could not do it justice here.

So if this is a topic you're interested in, just know that it does exist as a Demonolatry practice and there are many ways to honor and work with the Demons aligned with death. Also see the Demonolatry Funeral Rite in this book.

# Hymns

This section has been included because so many people have wondered about the words to hymns. The following hymns can be found at Lulu.com on the OFS exclusive CD, *ABYSS: Daemonolatry Hymns for Ritual & Meditation.* The following are spelt phoenetically where the actual words are unknown.

I learned the hymns from my teacher (by listening to her sing them), and she learned them from her father, who learned them from his teacher, and on down the line. To my knowledge, the only one we can link to any family grimoire or journal is Meleus De Quo Magna, which is basically a hymn to the nature of our universe and the magick (connection to us) within.

Others are simply hymns sung in praise to honor certain Demons (as in those to Leviathan and Lucifer) or to bless an event as in the Liturgy of Love, usually sung or played at Demonolatry marriage ceremonies. The

Meditations are exactly that. Singing or vibrating the hymns are condusive to deep meditation, and helpful prior to ascension. Enns can be used in this Hymn or vibratory manner, too.

## Meleus De Quo Maga

Prodere foras
quo numen de magicus
ad- mihi ejus
neus veneficium.

## Rite To Lucifer

Nas vocare tu Lucifer,
Parcepts es hic ritus.

## Ave Rege Leviathan

Ave rege Leviathan
Es mae na equi requiem
Alle man tre daray nas
Enae ave Satanas

## Liturgy of Love

Ananae broc ananae broc
An Rosier nanae sed
Aneva Ashtaroth reda gipe
An Astarte for nae ed.

## Earth Meditations

Ave na terra na terra na eva ta na
Ave na arhimon arhimon eva ta na
Ave na dagon dagon eva ta na

## Meditation

A-na nas pa na day
Eva ro –no Sata-na-an-ae

# Moving Onward

The questionnaires and this section have been included because many Demonolators seek to have a guideline by which to measure their knowledge and growth in the practice of Demonolatry. Without this guideline, many feel they are at a stalemate and cannot see the progress they're making in their quest for knowledge of themselves, relationships with the Demons, and ultimately their connection to all that is, Satan.

In addition to using the questionnaires, all Demonolators should keep journals of their practices, experiences, and spiritual epiphanies. It is so much easier to see how we've grown when we can go back and see where we started.

Traditionally, Demonolators only do advancement, degree advancement, or title giving rites of passage once the individual has reached a defined state of progress within the tradition. This means that traditionally, self or group initiations are only done after the pre-initiate questionnaire can be answered in full and the student has a strong knowledge of the topics in contains. Just as an adepthood rite should only be done when the initiate quesitonairre can be answered in full, and each subject elaborated on with detail and confidence.

## Using the Questionairres

These are the actual questionnaires used by members of the priesthood when deciding who will be initiated or moved ahead in title or status within a group. For the solitary practitioner, they can be helpful as a guideline to where you may need further study. Be honest with yourself when answering them.

Within a group setting, you are asked to elaborate on the answers as necessary as if you were explaining each concept. This is so the priest or priestess can determine whether or not the pre-initiate or initiate really understands the material.

### Pre-Initiate Training

How long have you been practicing Demonolatry?

Which of the following have you read?
> The Egyptian Book of the Dead
> The Hermetica
> Initiation into Hermetics
> The Hermetica – Lost Wisdom of the Pharohs
> Modern Demonolatry
> Lessons in Demonolatry

Which of the following areas of occult study or traditions have you studied before?
> Thelema

Luciferianism
Modern Satanism
Theistic Satanism
Goetic Magick
Ceremonial Magick
Sex Magick
Enochian Magick
Egyptian Religion and Magick (Khemetics)
Wicca
Witchcraft
Chaos Magick
Elemental Magick
Alchemy
Other: _____

Have you belonged to any of the following groups? If so, what degrees did you achieve?
OTO
Golden Dawn
AMORC
Temple of Set
Other: _____

Please answer the following questions to the best of your ability. Take your time. If you answer yes, please qualify your yes answer with an example or explanation. You can test out of any section if you feel you understand it well enough. Please indicate the sections you would like to test out of.

- Do you feel you understand basic Hermetics?
- Do you feel you understand the design of God and Deity?
- Can you see how Hermetic Science can be applied to Religion?

- Do you know how Hermetic Science works when it comes to Magickal Operations?
- What is your view of Demons? What are they? What are their personalities like?
- Do you understand the polarity of Demons?
- Do you understand how one Demon can become two?
- What Demonic Pantheons are you familiar with?
- Do you feel you understand the basics of Demonolatry?
- Are you familiar with Sect Law? If so, please summarize, in a sentence, what this means.
- Do you completely understand offerings?
- Do you regularly meditate?
- Do you know what prayer is and how to pray?
- Do you understand the basic parts of ritual?
- Are you familiar with the ritual implements?
- Do you understand the reasoning behind circle construction?

- Can you construct a circle without help?
- Do you understand the basic method of Demonolatry invocation (DZ)?
- Do you understand the purposes of the ritual tools and their symbolism?
- Do you know what ritual follow-up is?
- Have you chosen a matron/patron? If yes, which Demon and why?
- If yes, have you done a Dedication rite? If yes, please describe your experience with that.
- Do you know the difference between baptism and initiation?

Finally –

- Why did you choose Demonolatry?
- What particular areas of study are you interested in?

### Initiate Questionnaire:

- Do you understand your own fire make-up?
- Do you understand the various hermetic/alchemical aspects of fire?
- Do you understand the symbolism of fire?
- Do you know how to recognize and correct a fire imbalance?
- Do you understand which ritual tools are associated with fire?
- Can you identify at least five Demons associated with fire?
- Do you understand ceremonial magick?
- Do you understand the fire aspects of Enochian Magick?
- Do you understand the first two aspects of the tree of life and can you apply them to your current spiritual path?

- Do you understand your own water make-up?
- Do you understand the various hermetic/alchemical aspects of water?
- Do you understand the symbolism of water?
- Do you know how to recognize and correct a water imbalance?
- Do you understand which ritual tools are associated with water?
- Can you identify at least five Demons associated with water?

- Have you read any of the various ceremonial magick grimoires?
- Do you understand the water aspects of Enochian Magick?
- Do you understand the third and fourth aspects of the tree of life and can you apply them to your current spiritual path?

- Do you understand your own earth make-up?
- Do you understand the various hermetic/alchemical aspects of earth?
- Do you understand the symbolism of earth?
- Do you know how to recognize and correct a earth imbalance?
- Do you understand which ritual tools are associated with earth?
- Can you identify at least five Demons associated with earth?
- Do you understand Gematria and its use in magick and can you apply it to Demonolatry?
- Do you understand the earth aspects of Enochian Magick?
- Do you understand the fifth and sixth aspects of the tree of life and can you apply them to your current spiritual path?

- Do you understand your own air make-up?
- Do you understand the various hermetic/alchemical aspects of air?
- Do you understand the symbolism of air?
- Do you know how to recognize and correct a air imbalance?
- Do you understand which ritual tools are associated with air?

- Can you identify at least five Demons associated with air?
- Do you understand the air aspects of Enochian Magick?
- Do you understand the seventh and eighth aspects of the tree of life and can you apply them to your current spiritual path?

- Do you know what being an adept entails? (i.e. what is expected of you?)

## Determining Titles, Degrees, and Status

Aside from passing out questionnaires to students, members of the priesthood, or adept teachers might also have practitioners perform prescribed rituals and share their results. They may be given verbal or written tests. There are also questionnaires and tests given to adepts who wish to move on to the priesthood.

## The Priesthood

Traditionally the Demonolatry Priesthood treats the bloodline of the individual as one consideration for acceptance into training for the priesthood. But that does not necessarily apply in some modern groups. However, modern Demonolatry sects are still very selective about who they choose for priesthood training.

Some universal requirements for being accepted into the training for the traditional Demonolatry priesthood (assisting) include:

- Have been practicing Demonolatry for a minimum of six years.
- Have attained an Adept Status and have been Adept for a minimum of three years.
- Good people skills.
- Strong Empathy.
- Good organizational skills.
- Actively participates in worship and ritual both with the group and alone. (i.e. gets his/her hands dirty).
- Is an effective teacher.
- Possesses leadership skills.
- Has experience to draw from to counsel others.

As I said, these seem to be some of the universal requirements. Not so universal are the requirements of how long the person must have belonged to the particular group, which rites, enns, and prayers can be recited from memory. The ability to create ritual from scratch. Deep understanding of the symbolism behind all aspects of the ritual work. And so on.

Basically, in traditional Demonolatry, few if any people are just handed a priesthood title and no one can just declare themselves a priest. There is no entitlement. The title has to be earned and it takes years of study, training, dedication to spiritual growth of the self and others, and the ability to lead and guide others.

More importantly, not everyone is fit for the priesthood. Some Demonolators have practiced for years and are content to remain Adept because they have no desire to really lead and deal with people. Instead, they may pick and choose students to teach, or merely concentrate on themselves and their own spiritual work, which is wonderful. In knowing themselves they have made that correct choice. Others are not suited by personality. For example, the person whose sought after advice to a student's external life problems is apathetic and goes something like, "Get over it", "Deal with it" or "Your divorce is not my problem and shouldn't affect you spiritually, so buck up and get back to work on those rituals I gave you," is likely not a good candidate.

So before you aspire to the priesthood, ask yourself why. Do you truly wish to help others (with advice and counseling) along their own path (divorces and all), or are you seeking the title and power? It's not about the title and good priests do not bask in the glow of self-righteousness nor the condemnation of others. Being a priest has nothing to do with preaching the word of Satan so-to-speak, because Satan may have different words for each of us to help us along our individual paths to a spiritual gnosis. Also, in a sect led by a proper priest, the decision-making for the whole group is often done after the adepts (and sometimes initiates) of the group have been consulted for their input. So priests do not have, and should not have, infinite power over others under ther charge.

So be honest with yourself. It takes far more than a deep love and reverence for the Demons to seek the Demonolatry Priesthood. There are other people involved who have real problems, emotions, and lives to wrestle with along with their own spiritual growth. The true priest understands this and will help their group members as much as they can, even if that help or advice means telling the person to take a break from ritual or group work to reflect on and solve the external (outside Demonolatry) life problems they may be experiencing. Even if a member is absent to concentrate on other issues, the priest will check up on the member to see if she is okay. It is for this reason that traditional groups are extremely cautious in who they choose to accept for training, let alone ordainment.

Besides, worshipping the Demons and growing spiritually has nothing to do with titles. The titles are there as rites of passage to acknowledge the work and growth of the individual. Priests exist merely to lead a group in ritual and keep the group together as well as teaching neophytes and guiding others along individual spiritual pathwork.

Also remember the Courtesies and that we are all on equal footing. We should not use our titles to lord over others, or to brag that any one title indicates one person is better or more special than another.

That being said, I wasn't going to re-include the Priesthood questionnaire examples that were included in Lessons in Demonolatry. Then I realized that was terribly unfair of me. Why should I withhold that information when I shared it freely before. It will be of no use (other than to satisfy curiosity) to those who do not belong to a group or who do not aspire to the priesthood.

Then it occurred to me that this book will be used by members of groups who might want this type of information because they do aspire to the priesthood. So I rethought that decision and the following are the examples of the types of Questionairres the clergy might use to assess the readiness of a member for priesthood training. These obviously aren't the same questionnaires groups use. They are simply samples of the types of questions a candidate for the priesthood might be expected to know the answers to (on many levels). Who knows – perhaps some of the questions will give you something to ponder, and in the process you could have a deep or profound realization.

# Sample Qualification Exam for the Assisting Priesthood.

Who is Aleister Crowley and what has he contributed to Demonolatry? What did Demonolatry contribute to him?

How many families are in the Dukanté hierarchy?

Please list the purpose for each family and explain why they are broken into families.

What type of religion is Demonolatry and how does it differ from Christianity - theologically?

Please do the following: Construct a circle, light a purple candle, and meditate on the flame until the candle is extinguished. What did this exercise teach you?

Please list the nine Demonic divinities and their relationships to one another as well as the reasoning behind the concept of the divinities.

Please explain how ritual tools are consecrated and how often a sect-assisting priest(ess) should perform this task.

What is your primary purpose toward your fellow sect members as an assisting priest(ess)?

## PRESIDING PRIEST(ESS)' NOTES

Can the adept construct a circle and recite the appropriate enns from memory?

Can the adept perform a ritual in proper order?

Is the adept familiar with Sect Law and does (s)he exibit this knowledge?

# Sample Qualification Exam for the Priesthood

*This is often a verbal test. The priest or priestess must administer the verbal exam. (Note: the answers to these questions cannot be found in any text and no priest or priestess will give you the answers - only the tools by which to gain them.)*

How many years have you been a practicing Demonolator?

How many years have you studied the occult?

Please list the traditions you have studied and feel you have an understanding of?

Define the Demon entity and the concept of deity.

If you were to do a rite in absence of a ritual circle, what happens?

Elaborate rites such as those outlined in the Grand Grimoire, Grimorium Verum, Goetic Rituals, and the like have specific instructions that must be followed exactly. Why?

Please take the Demon Delepitoré into consideration. In the Dukanté hierarchy, she is the Demoness of Magick and is a member of the first family. What does this tell us about her elemental, hourly, and planetary correspondences?

How does magick/sorcery work?

In Dukanté's rite to Ascend to the Demonic Plane he states that one should travel through caverns of darkness and face his/her fears one by one and he would ascend to the Demonic plane. Crowley had a similar exercise. How is this rite done and what is its purpose?

What is the purpose of symbol during ritual? What do symbols have to do with magick?

What is a ritual/rite/or ceremony?

What do Demons, a flower, and a fingernail all have in common?

Please respond to the following items with explanations and/or your thoughts. Each is an actual message that a real Demonolator was given by a Demonic entity.

> a. Great succubus walk with the moon, that which is hidden shall reveal secrets soon.
> b. The plane you seek is not far from your own existence.
> c. Every rite you encounter has something wrong with it.

List the powers of sorcery and explain how each one relates to the rest.

List the courtesies and their importance.

For each elemental direction give the Demon(s), the element, planetary correspondences, and enn. Then, please explain in some detail how they all work together.

What is an Enn and how does it work?

How many spiritual realizations have you had during your time as a Demonolator?

How long was your dedication ritual and to whom did you do it? Did you have any spiritual experiences during or after the rite?

What has being a Demonolator meant to you and has it changed your perspective? If so, how?

## PRESIDING PRIEST(ESS)' NOTES

Is the AP able to conduct formal ceremonies from memory?

Is the AP able to construct a circle with ease and fluidity and the ability to recite the enns from memory?

Has the AP taken basic psychology and counseling/intervention classes?

Does the AP work well with people?

Can the AP effectively answer questions about spiritual matters so that people understand her?

Can the AP draw the blood of another person?

Can the AP take on students and effectively mentor them?

# Concluding Thoughts

After you've finished working through this book, and you wish to more deeply explore the various practices of Demonolatry, there are books out there that discuss more specific Demonolatry topics.

Remember the courtesies and may your worship of the Demons bring you enlightenment and growth always. Naamah.

# Basic Oleum Recipes

## Directions for making bases and other oils.

Virgin Olive oil is most often used because it has very little scent. Mix together equal parts (unless specified) until you have one to three cups depending on the amount of oil you need. Add enough oil to make a mush, heat in a bowl in a pan of hot water. When it begins to boil, add more oil. Boil for ten minutes, and strain through cheesecloth. Place in jars, add tincture of benzoin or 100 proof alcohol for preservation.

## *Base Oil for Oleums and Salves*

### Selinda's Favorite BASE
Pure Virgin Olive Oil
Parsley
Celery Root
Cinquefoil
Mandrake
Poppy
Vervain
Patchouli
Tincture of Benzoin - four drops per 2 drams

### BASE #1
Pure Virgin Olive Oil
Sandalwood
Orris Root
Thyme
Poppy Seed
Myrrh
Frankincense
Tincture of Benzoin - four drops per 2 drams

### BASE #2
Pure Virgin Olive Oil
Hemlock *(poisonous!)*
Wormwood
Cornsilks
Optional: Colestrom Formulae
Tincture of Benzoin - four drops per 2 drams

### BASE #3
Pure Virgin Olive Oil
Wild Celery
Poplar Leaves
Sweet Birch

Tincture of Benzoin - four drops per 2 drams

**BASE #4 (recommended)**
Pure Virgin Olive Oil
Wormwood
Cinquefoil
Wild Celery
Poplar Leaves (optional)
Soot (if salve - optional)
Tincture of Benzoin - four drops per 2 drams


**INITIATION BASE**
Pure Virgin Olive Oil
Catnip
Sandalwood
Frankincense
Myrrh
Tincture of Benzoin - four drops per 2 drams

**Tincture of Benzoin**
1 part Benzoin finely ground
3 parts alcohol


**Oleum of Rosier**
Base
Cinnimon
Cloves
Ginger
Lavender
Roses
Dragon's Blood
Cardamom

**Oleum of Leviathan**
Base
Calamus
Ground solar sea salt
1 tsp Rain/River Water

**Oleum of Verrine**
Base
Bayberry
Mullberry
Dragons Blood
Camphor

**Oleum of Lucifer**
Base
Poppy
Lemon
Alum - just a pinch
Black Mustard

**Oleum of Belial**
Base
Vetivert
Patchouli
Sandalwood
Cedar

**Oleum of Flereous**
Base
Rue
Arnica
Dragon's Blood

**Oleum of Belphegore**
Base
Patchouli

Lemon Balm
Sandalwood
Gum Arabic

**Tezrian Plague**
One cup olive juice
1 teaspoon Olive oil (optional)
3 types of perfumed plants of your choice (I use roses,
lavender, and gladiola's)
1/2 cup alcohol

**Black Paper Squares for large rituals**. These parchment
squares are used to write requests on and are then burned.
Fun for the whole Sect!

- 2x2 Parchment squares
- Controlling Oil
- Melted Black Wax

Make **controlling oil** by steeping Calamus and
Hemlock in olive oil as the recipe calls for it. Store in cool,
dark place for three weeks.

Place parchment squares (as many as will be
needed) in controlling oil. Heat oven to low bake. Place
squares on cookie sheets. Bake for 5 minutes and cool. Dip
one at a time into the hot wax using a tweezer. Cool until
wax hardens. Store in a box to be placed on the altar.

# Bibliography & Suggested Reading

Ashley, Leonard R.N., *The Complete Book of Devils and Demons* 1996 Barricade Books, New York

Ashwin, E. A.; Translator ,*Compendium Maleficarum* 1988 Dover Publications, New York

Barrett, Francis, *The Magus* 1989 Citadel Press, New York

Baskin, Wade, *Satanism* 1991 Carol Publishing Group, New York

Bardon, Franz *Initiation Into Hermetics*

Budge, E. A. Wallace, *The Egyptian Book of the Dead*

Connolly, S. *Art of Creative Magick, The*, 2005 DB Publishing.

Connolly, S. (Editor, Various Authors) *Demonolatry Rites*, 2005, DB Publishing

Connolly, S. *Lessons in Demonolatry*, 2005 DB Publishing

Connolly, S. *Modern Demonolatry*, First Printing 1999 Darkerwood Publishing Group, Second Printing 2005, DB Publishing.

Dukanté, Richard , *The Dukanté Grimoires* Not Published

Freke & Gandy, *The Hermetica: Lost Wisdom of the Pharoahs*

Guiley, Rosemary Ellen *The Encyclopedia of Witches and Witchcraft* 1989 Facts on File, New York

Hermes Trismegistus, *The Hermetica*

Hyatt, Victoria & Charles, Joseph W. *The Book of Demons* 1974 Simon and Schuster, New York

Joseph, Isya *Devil Worship* 1997 Kessinger Publishing Co., Montana USA

Kieckhefer, Richard *Forbidden Rites* 1997 Pennsylvania State University Press, PA

Kohl, Benjamin G. and Midelfort, H.C. Erik Editors *On Witchcraft; an abridged Translation of Johan Weyer's De Praestigiis Daemonum* 1998 Pegasus Press, North Carolina

LaVey, Anton Szandor *The Satanic Bible* 1969 Avon Books, New York

LaVey, Anton Szandor *The Satanic Rituals* 1972 Avon Books, New York

Marwick, Max; Editor *Witchcraft & Sorcery* 1987 Penguin Books, New York

Mathers, S.L. MacGregor *The Key of Solomon the King: Clavicula Salomonis*, 1992 Samuel Weiser, York Beach, ME

Mathers, S.L. MacGregor; Translator *The Goetia*: *The Lesser Key of Solomon* 1997 Samuel Weiser, York Beach Maine

Mathers, S.L. MacGregor; Translator *The Grimoire of Armadel* 1998 Samuel Weiser, York Beach, ME

Parker, John *At the Heart of Darkness* 1993 Citadel Press, New York

Paulsen, Kathryn *Magic & Witchcraft* 1980 Penguin Books, New York

Purswell, Ellen *Goetic Demonolatry*, 2005 DB Publishing.

Purswell, Grant *The Purswell Family Grimoires* Not Published

Remy, Nicolas *Demonolatry* 1930 John Rodker, London

Seleneicthon *Daemonic Magick* 1994 Mi-World Publishing, Florida

Seleneicthon *Gods, Spirits, Daemons* 1994 Mi-World Publishing, Florida

Spence, Lewis *An Encyclopedia of Occultism* 1993 Citidel Press, New York

Summers, Montague *The History of Witchcraft* 1993 Carol Publishing Group, New Jersey

Summers, Montague; Translator *The Malleus Maleficarum* 1971 Dover Publications, New York

Waite, Arthur Edward *The Book of Black Magic* 1991 Samuel Weiser, York Beach, Maine

Whitcomb, Bill *The Magician's Companion* 1993 Llewellyn Publications, St. Paul MN

Willit, Alexander *The Willit Family Grimoires*   Not Published

**OTHERS:**

*Grimoirium Verum* 1997 Trident Books, Seattle Washington

*The Grand Grimoire* 1996 Trident Books/Ars Obscura, Seattle Washington

*Dr. Faustus* , Christopher Marlowe, 1604.

*The Divine Comedy* - Dante Algeheri, 1300.

# INDEX

## N

## O

## P

## Q

## R

## S

# OTHER BOOKS FROM DB Publishing

### Books By Demonolators For Demonolators™

- ◊ Abyss: Demonolatry Hymns for Ritual & Meditation
- ◊ Art of Creative Magick
- ◊ Complete Book of Demonolatry
- ◊ Demonolatry Rites
- ◊ Goetic Demonolatry
- ◊ Honoring Death
- ◊ Meditation Journal
- ◊ Ritus Record Libri
- ◊ Satanic Clergy Manual
- ◊ Kasdeya Rite of Ba'al

**To see a complete list of our titles and authors, visit our Online Store at:** http://www.ofs-demonolatry.org/bookstore.htm

**Or visit our Lulu shop pages at:**

Page 1 – http://www.lulu.com/demonolatry/
Page 2 – http://www.lulu.com/demonolatry2/

You may also contact us directly for bulk discounts, distribution to small bookstores, or ordering our titles with money order by writing to ofs.admin@gmail.com .

Made in the USA
Las Vegas, NV
04 October 2024

96309785R00223